Islamic
Corporate Banking

Mike Nagavalli

Mohamed Mahari

Introduction

There are many books out there related to Islamic Banking and Shariah (also spelled Sharia) law including, of course, the ubiquitous "book for dummies". A Google search about Islamic Banking literally returns hundreds of thousands of hits, which provide endless articles and opinions about Islamic Finance.

So, why this book? Well, for four main reasons:

First and foremost, we wanted to write a book specifically about Islamic Banking from a Corporate Transaction Banking or Wholesale Transaction Banking perspective. The objective of this book is to inform corporate treasurers, corporate managers and corporate bankers the fundamental difference between conventional corporate banking products typically used by Corporations v/s their Islamic counterparts. We also want to point out why corporate managers may want to consider Islamic banking products over conventional products. So, the scope of this book is limited to Islamic corporate transaction banking and could be considered a *specialized* book. Even though we will briefly touch on retail or consumer banking, most of the topics covered in this book relate to corporate transaction banking.

The second reason is that, even though there are many books out there about Islamic Banking, most of them are quite expensive and probably out of reach for many casual readers. There are indeed some books that are very affordable, but these cover a broad range of topics and do not specifically cover corporate banking. We want to make this book very specific and very detailed about corporate transaction banking and very affordable so it will be within reach for most people.

The third reason is that most of the books talk about Islamic products in general terms and do not go into details. Most book cover the Islamic products from a legal construct point of view but not do not detail the step-by-step process of how these products work. In addition, most books do not highlight the fundamental differences between Conventional products and their counterparts in Islamic. In this book we highlight the differences between the two as well as point out the pros and cons under each.

The fourth reason is to point out that over the past few decades conventional banking or traditional banking (which has its roots in free or mixed market-based economies) and Islamic banking (which is based on Shariah law) are converging and moving closer and closer together. Imagine if you will, conventional banking being on the extreme left and Islamic banking on the extreme right. What we have seen over the past few decades is that both sides from their respective positions are moving towards the center.

Because the free or mixed market economies believe that less government and less regulation is best, they rely on self-policing or market forces as a control mechanism. However, lack of controls over the past several decades led to some illegal or unregulated practices which in turn led to recessions or market collapses. This in turn forced these economies to implement new regulations to control or curb such practices. Indeed, this may seem ironic from a free-market philosophy perspective, but with such regulations the free-market economies are becoming regulated economies indeed.

Likewise, even though Islamic banking enforces a strict compliance to the principles of Shariah law, over the past few decades we have seen a less strict interpretation of Shariah law which has enabled adoption of traditional banking products to work under Shariah law with some modifications.

There may be very different philosophical views between conventional banking and Islamic banking, but as we will point out in this book, there are positives and negatives in both. If recent trends are indeed an indication of things to come, it appears that the mixed market economics are adopting stricter regulations mimicking some of the Shariah principles while Islamic banking is opening to some of the mixed market principles.

In this book you will find a detailed description of how Islamic Banking products are structured differently from their conventional or traditional counterparts. More importantly, we will cover why they are structured differently. Understanding the "why" will provide good insights into some of the protections that Islamic banking products offer over their conventional counterparts. By understanding the why, it is our hope that you will consider Islamic products in addition to conventional products and build up a portfolio of both.

Note: One of the common myths out there is that Islamic banking products are only for use by Muslims or Corporates that are registered in Muslim countries. This is not true. Islamic banking products may be used by anyone or any Corporate anywhere in the world as long as there are banks that offer them. Many banks and corporations around the world are realizing this and are including Islamic products in their portfolio.

But, before we delve into Islamic banking, let us first go through a brief overview of Islam and Shariah law.

Disclaimer: the descriptions and the step-by-step details about Islamic products in this book are generic in nature. Sometimes different Shariah boards in different countries have different interpretations which impacts the applicability of certain products or the processes involved in operating these products in their countries. Therefore, it is highly recommended that one should check within each specific country what products or processes are applicable.

A Brief Introduction to Islam

Islam is the second largest religion in the world with over 1 billion followers. It is a religion based on a faith in one supreme God, Allah. The people who believe in Islam are known as Muslims.

The Quran, the holy book of Islam, guides every Muslim in the way to live their lives and in their business practices. The Quran is a compilation of God's revelations to the Prophet Muhammad beginning in the year 609 when Prophet Muhammad was 40 years old. Muslims consider Prophet Muhammad as the last prophet of God.

God is said to have revealed to Prophet Muhammad through the angel Gabriel the concept of one God and about the ways to worship him and about the ways to live a better life. These revelations were given over a period of 23 years and in the beginning were recited from memory by Prophet Muhammad to his followers. After Muhammad's death, these recitations were compiled into a holy book called the Quran. The Quran in Arabic literally means "the recitation". The Quran is considered the unchanged word of God and is also considered as the constitution and the guide for Muslims in this life.

In addition to the Quran, also important are the traditions and the sayings and the actions of Prophet Muhammad. These are collectively called the "Hadith" or the "Sunnah". Thus the Quran and the Hadith together comprise the holy books of Islam.

Islam is an Arabic word, which means "submission". This reflects the faith's central doctrine of submitting to the will of God. The religion Islam not only covers the spiritual aspects but also covers material (trade or business) and moral (behavioral) aspects. Thus, the tenets of Islam not only cover religion but also cover the way of business and life.

Every follower of Islam believes in this central doctrine and is expected to follow the Islamic way of life from a spiritual, material and moral point of view.

The Concept of Islam

The concept of Islam is based on three basic elements:
- a) The articles of beliefs or faith known as Aqidah
- b) A set of moral codes known as Akhlaq
- c) A set of principles and laws known as Shariah

In this book we will touch briefly on Aqidah and Akhlaq to provide context. The main focus of this book will be on Shariah since Islamic Banking is based on the principles found in the Shariah. The Shariah principles and laws govern how people conduct their business, their lives and their behavior.

Thus, Shariah not only covers the legal (the jurisprudence) but also covers practices related to personal behaviors such as social interactions and business.

The following diagram (Figure 1) depicts the classification of Islam showing where Islamic Banking fits in which is the main focus of this book.

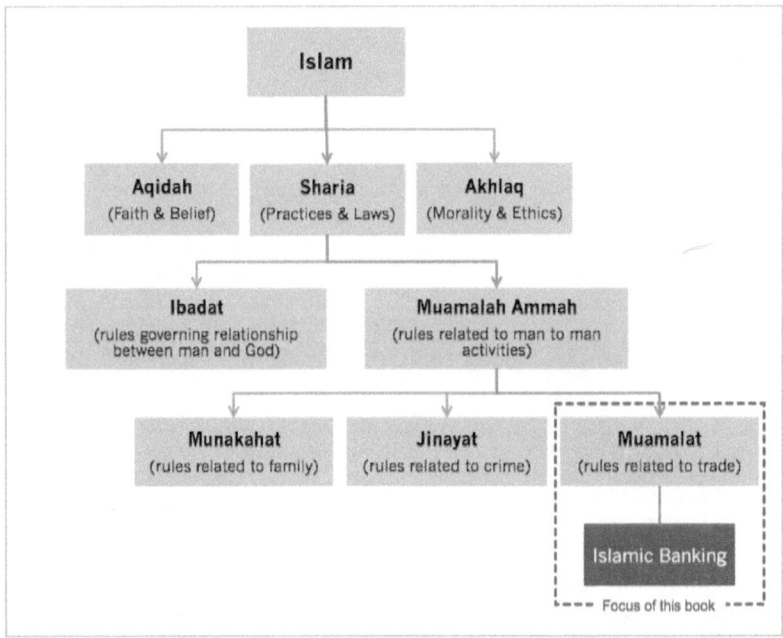

Figure 1

Since the objective of this book is on Islamic banking and finance, most of our focus will be on the Shariah component, which is where the Muamalat rules are found that govern the commercial transactions. However, as mentioned earlier, we will briefly touch on other components in order to provide an overall context of Islam.

Aqidah - the articles and beliefs of Faith

One of the key elements of Islam is the Aqidah; the six articles of faith & belief. These six articles of faith and belief are derived from the Quran and Sunnah and all Muslims are obligated to accept them. Both the Shias and the Sunnis, the two predominant sects in Islam, accept these articles without question even though there may be some differences in their belief system.

Note: the following brief description of this classification is from www.takafuleexam.com:

The six articles of belief or faith are:

1. Belief in One God (Allah)

Islam is a monotheistic religion and the belief that there is only one God is fundamental to the faith. The idea of multiple gods is rejected in Islam as emphasized many times in the Quran, such as in this verse:

2. Belief in the Angels

Muslims believe in the existence of angels, which are special beings mentioned numerous times in the Quran. God has created angels to carry on special duties that He has decreed on them. Although angels are beings that cannot be seen by humans, the Quran makes it clear that every Muslim should believe in their existence.

3. Belief in the Prophets

Muslims believe that since the beginning of mankind, God has sent a long line of prophets and messengers to convey the message of monotheism to the world. The first of these prophets was Adam and the last was Prophet Muhammad who has a special status in Islam because he is believed to be the final prophet and he received the revelation of the Quran.

4. Belief in the Scriptures

Muslims have high reverence for the Torah, the Psalms and the Gospel. These books are believed to be God's message that was revealed to the prophets before Muhammad. However, Muslims believe that these books have been altered over the centuries. The Quran was sent down to correct the mistakes in the previous books and serve as the perfect guidance for mankind until the world comes to an end. God promises that the purity of the Quran is protected for eternity.

5. Belief in the Day of Judgment and Afterlife
Muslims believe that, on the Day of Judgment, each individual will be held accountable for every action that he or she has committed during the course of his or her life. On this day, every soul will be dealt with the utmost justice, as declared in the Quran:

We shall set up scales of justice for the Day of Judgment, so that not a soul will be dealt with unjustly in the least. (Quran 21:47)

6. Belief in Divine Decree
Islam teaches that God not only foreknows, but also foreordained all that comes to pass in the world and in the lives of individuals. Therefore, Muslims believe that although humans have the free will to make their own choices in life, everything that happens in life occurs only because of His Will and Knowledge.

The above six beliefs are the core of the Aqidah belief system. To demonstrate their faith in these principles, Muslims are required to learn the Quran and follow the examples set by Prophet Muhammad as put forth in the books of Hadith.

In addition to the above beliefs, there are five rules or obligations that all Muslims must also follow as stated in the Quran, which we will look at next.

The Five Requirements (Obligations) of Islam
In addition to the articles of belief, Muslims are obligated to practice the following which are known as the Five Obligations of Islam:

Shahada - is the testimony of faith in the fundamental belief in one God. Sincere recitation of confession of faith before two witnesses who are Muslims is the sole requirement for those who wish to join the Muslim community. It represents acceptance not only of Allah and his prophet but also of the entirety of Islam. As one of the Obligation, the Shahada must be recited correctly and aloud with full understanding and internal assent at least once in every Muslim's lifetime.

Salat –the Muslim prayer is the second of the five rules of Islam. Salat is performed five times a day: at dawn, midday, afternoon, sunset and evening. The person praying is required to face the direction of the Kaaba shrine located in Mecca. A prayer mat called sajjada, is commonly used during Salat. Salat may be performed individually or with other Muslims. The midday prayer on Fridays at mosques is the most important prayer of all.

Zakat – charity giving to help the poor and needy is a central requirement in Islam. The Quran explicitly requires it and often places it alongside prayer when discussing a Muslim's duties.

Sawm - fasting during the month of Ramadan. During Ramadan, all adult Muslims are required to abstain from food, drink or any sexual activity during daylight hours.

Hajj - pilgrimage to Mecca. Every Muslim is expected to undertake a pilgrimage to Mecca, the sacred city of Islam, at least once in their lifetime. This pilgrimage is called the hajj in Arabic. While a visit to Mecca is beneficial any time of the year, it must take place during the month of the last month of the Islamic year (Dhu al-Hijja) to fulfill the requirements of the hajj.

The Akhlaq – set of Moral codes

Akhlaq refers to virtue and morality which are believed to be good behavior, good disposition, good conduct, good nature, temper, ethics, morals or character of a person. That is, it refers to a person's nature or core being.

Islam believes that a person can acquire either good character or bad character based on their will and practice. In Islam it is important not only to believe in faith but also to practice the moral values. One cannot be a good believer of faith and a not a good practitioner of the moral code. Both of these go hand in hand.

A person can be a good practitioner of faith (performing ritual acts of worship, praying in the mosque, reciting lots of verses from Quran, and so forth) but not necessarily a good practitioner of moral values. This person cannot be considered a good Muslim. In Islam, there is no such thing as a good Muslim but a bad person. To be a good Muslim one must be a good person.

Shariah - a set of Principles and Laws

Shariah means "a way" or "a path". It is the legal framework regulating the public and private lives of those living in a legal system based on Shariah. Shariah deals with all aspects of day-to-day life, including politics, economics, banking, business and contract law and social issues. Thus, Shariah law is comprehensive in nature since it provides all the laws necessary for a person's spiritual and physical well-being.

In general, the Shariah laws are derived from the Quran and the Hadith or Sunnah. We already discussed that the Quran is recitations from God as revealed to Prophet Muhammad. Hadith, on the other hand, refers to the way Prophet Muhammad lived his life; that is, his sayings, his acts, his behaviors, the way he performed the prayer, the fasting, the ritual of hajj, or the commercial transactions he concluded, etc. Taken together, these are known as the primary sources of Shariah laws (refer Figure 2 below).

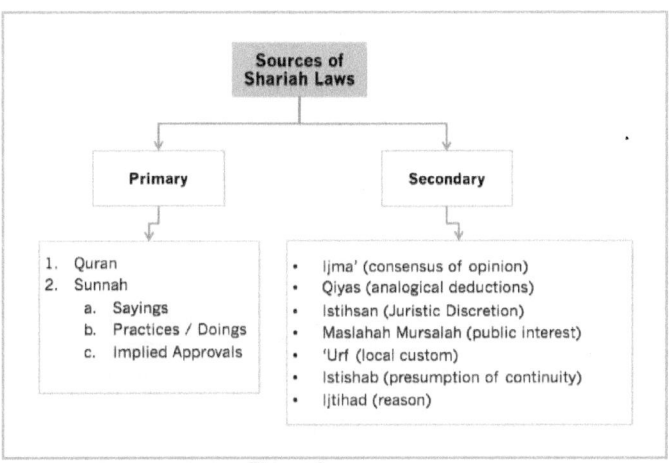

Figure 2

In addition to the primary sources, several secondary sources also exist (see above). The most common among the secondary sources are Ijma and Qiyas.

Ijma refers to the unanimous agreement amongst the mujtahidun - the scholars who have the authority to make judgments on questions that are not covered in the Quran or the Hadith or are subject to interpretation.

Qiyas refers to analogy or applicability of rulings established in earlier cases on the current case. In a conventional sense, this is akin to the applicability of any precedence to the current case.

As mentioned earlier, Muamalat, which deals with principles of commercial and financial transactions, is part of Shariah laws which we will look at next.

Principles of Muamalat (or transactions)

Under conventional market driven economies, a well functioning financial system is critical to a successful economic engine. A system where the price of the goods and services is set by supply and demand and where the buyers and sellers are free to find each other through marketplaces is crucial to a well functioning market economy.

Likewise, a well functioning economy based on the above principles is also crucial under Islamic economic system. However, in Islamic economic system, it is also crucial that the economic system conforms to the Shariah principles.

Because conformity to Shariah principles is a very important part of every business transaction under Islamic economic system, understanding these principles is important in order to appreciate the rationale behind this system.

Economic objectives and non-economic objectives are an important part of the Islamic financial system. Economic objectives such as, private ownership, profit motive, prices driven by supply and demand and accumulation of wealth are part of the Islamic financial system. However, non-economic objectives such as ban on interest and ban on unlawful goods and services and ban on speculation are also part and parcel of the Islamic financial system. The non-economic objectives are considered restrictions imposed by divinity and therefore cannot be changed by humans. Economic and non-economic objectives work together in the Islamic economic system in providing a balanced approach to wealth distribution and equality in opportunities.

The principles of Muamalat or commercial and financial transactions are broken down into desirable activities and obligatory activities. Those that are desirable are enforced via education; those that are obligatory are enforced by law.

Desirable Principles of Muamalat

Permissibility. This rule assumes that all transactions are valid as it is expected that all transactions conform to the principles of Shariah, unless there is evidence that a transaction has broken the principles of Shariah.

When dealing in day-to-day dealings, one may generally assume that transactions conform to Shariah principles and are valid. But one must be careful. If it is discovered that a transaction has broken the principles of Shariah, the transaction may be declared invalid at any time after the transaction was completed.

Therefore, it is always better to seek advice and approval of Shariah Boards if a new product or service is introduced, or a specific bespoke contract is signed. This is like seeking advice from legal experts prior to finalizing a contract in conventional finance.

Contracts by mutual consents. This rule ensures that the contracts entered by the parties involved were concluded without any coercion, fraud, misrepresentation or by any other legal means. If a contract was later determined that it did not follow this rule, it could be deemed null and void.

Transparency. All transactions (commercial and financial) must be conducted with full transparency. That is, all parties know about the important facts about the transaction including the cost, the profit margin, and the terms and conditions.

Wide Circulation of Wealth. Profit and wealth should be distributed among the general populace. Hoarding or accumulation of wealth by individuals is discouraged.

Fair Dealing. Fair dealing or justice must always be observed in all Islamic transactions or contracts.

Compulsory Principles of Muamalat

In the previous section we have seen the *desirable* principles of Muamalat. Now we look at compulsory principles. There are six compulsory principles of Muamalat in addition to the five desirable principles discussed above. Let's look at each one in detail.

Ban on Riba (i.e.: interest). In Arabic language Riba literally means "increment or addition". As such, this "increment" is generally associated with interest one would pay for loans or interest one would earn on deposits. For e.g.: If a lender provides a borrower with a loan for $100,000 at 5% interest per annum, after one year the borrower is required to pay back to the lender $105,000 ($100,000, called the principal amount, plus $5,000 in interest). If the term of the loan calls for a 2-year loan, the borrower is required to pay back a sum of $110,000 at the end of 2 years ($100,000 principal amount plus $10,000 in interest). This is assuming the loan was lent on a simple interest basis and not compounded and the loan is paid off in lump sum and not in monthly installments.

Likewise, under conventional banking, if someone deposits money into a savings account at a bank, the bank may pay interest to the depositor.

Interest earned this way is banned under Shariah. According to Shariah, one cannot make money just from lending money. In other words, money cannot be used by itself to make money. Money can only be made under real commercial activity.

Why is Interest Prohibited?

According to general interpretations of Shariah, earning money on money, where there is no productive activity or trade is not allowed. Also, since social injustice and unfairness are strictly prohibited in Shariah, interest is not allowed as lenders may unjustly profit from weak positions of borrowers.

The belief is that the interest system brings about a pattern of income distribution that is biased towards the wealthy and large businesses. The lenders may charge whatever interest they wish since the borrowers may be in a desperate situation to get financing. For example, this may be the case where someone is just getting started in business and has not established a "credit" history and is required to pay higher interest rates. Or it may be the case where someone is very desperate and is willing to pay whatever interest is being charged. In other words, the borrowers potentially could be at the mercy of the lenders leading to unjust practices.

In addition, it is believed that the interest-based system relinquishes the lenders of responsibilities and risks in investment activities. The lenders may not care how well the business venture is doing as long as they get paid. The lenders in interest- based systems worry about the borrower's ability to pay the lender and not necessarily the viability of the underlying business. For eg: a lender may accept a house as a collateral and provide a loan (eg: home equity loan). In this case, the lender may not be interested in what the borrower does with the money as long as the lender is assured that they will get their money back by selling the house if the borrower does not pay.

In other words, some lenders may only be interested in making sure they get their money back and are not really interested in what the money is used for. This sets up a system where the borrowers may be able to get financing even for high-risk business ventures by pledging everything they have and eventually losing everything they have. This then also may set up a pattern where the income distribution favors the rich and powerful who may unjustly profit from the weak position of the borrowers.

Based on recent events under conventional banking, most of us have seen many unjust practices by lenders. For example:

• Charging incredibly high interest rates on credit cards where the borrower has lower credit score or if a payment is missed by the borrower. Many global banks were charging or still charge 20% to 30% or more per annum interest rates on credit cards!

• Unscrupulous money lenders prey on desperate borrowers by taking jewelry or property as collateral and charging such high interest that most of the borrowers couldn't possibly pay off the loans and end up losing everything they have.

In contrast to this, even though Shariah does not allow interest (or Riba), it does allow profit making. However, profit making must come with taking risk in the business. This means the lender may be entitled to profit only if the lender is also willing to share the loss. In other words, the lenders must also have their "skin in the game"; they must be participants in the success or failure of the business venture into which they are lending their money.

Sharing responsibilities and sharing the risks is inherent in the profit/loss sharing methods of Islamic banking. An Islamic interest-free financial system supports a fair income distribution pattern where the risks and profits (or losses) from a business venture are shared by the lender and the borrower.

Because the lenders are also sharing the risk, it is believed that the lenders will be interested in learning more about the business venture and only lend money for business ventures that have a potential to be successful or help business succeed. This then sets up a pattern where both the lenders and borrowers become more successful and the income distribution is fair. It is believed this also eliminates the unjust practices of high interest rates and lenders praying upon desperate borrowers.

Sources and Types of Riba

There are two main sources of Riba and many types of Riba under each source. The main source of Riba is that which arises out of borrowing...i.e.: interest payments. The other source of Riba arises out of trade activities, i.e.: sales.

We have already covered the Riba arising from interest in the previous section. Let's now look at the Riba arising out of sales activities which includes the following:

Riba Jahiliyyah - any penalty imposed on the borrower in case of late payments is banned. Let's say the borrower fails to make the payment by the due date but makes it 15 days later. Under the conventional banking system, the bank charges a penalty typically called "late payment fee". This "penalty" is not allowed under Islamic finance as it conforms to the theory of making money on money which is not allowed.

However, in order to discourage borrowers from making late payments, the lenders may ask for "donations" which the lenders are obligated to donate to charities. The lenders cannot keep the money they get for donations.

Riba Fadhl occurs in the situation where unequal quantities (or qualities) of the same kind are exchanged. It is required that the trade must be like-for-like and equal-for-equal. For eg: one cannot borrow 1Kg of rice and return 1Kg of wheat (this is not like for like) or borrow 1kg of rice and return 2kg of rice (this is not equal for equal).

This concept is similar to the concept of "consideration" in conventional finance. Consideration is something of value given by a promisor to a promisee in exchange for something of value given by a promisee to a promisor. In other words, the things being exchanged must have some value in the eyes of the law, even though generally the legal system does not care by how much.

In conventional economies people are entitled and expected to determine the value of things for themselves. Consideration must be sufficient, but the law does not weigh in on the adequacy of consideration. Thus, if someone buys a Ferrari for $1 that would be perfectly fine under conventional systems as long as both the buyer and the seller agreed to the terms without coercion and as long as any taxes due are paid for the full value of the car and there is no money laundering or illegal activity involved.

However, under Shariah, for commodities that can be measured or weighed, like-for-like and equal-for-equal are important. These cannot be like-for-unlike and payment cannot be deferred. Shariah does indeed allow one to pay for rice with currency or gold or other acceptable commodities. However, in like-for-unlike transactions deferred payment is not allowed and payment must be made on the spot. For eg: if one is paying for rice using currency, the payment must be made on the spot.

Riba Buyu - occurs if unequal exchange of like-for-like commodity is transacted or future delivery date is involved. This is prohibited.

Ban on Uncertainty (Gharar). Uncertainty in any transaction is banned. This is related to the concept of full visibility and transparency and disclosure wherein all parties in a transaction must know exactly what the terms and conditions are including the quantity and quality and the price of what is being bought and sold. There should be no ambiguity, and nothing should be hidden from any of the parties in order to avoid unjust or unfair outcomes for some of the parties in a transaction. If Gharar exists, the contract or sale may become void.

There are two types of Gharar – minor (Yasir) and major (Fahish). Minor Gharar normally does not void the contract if it does not affect the main elements of the contract.

Fahish (major Gharar), on the other hand, means the uncertainty affects the core elements of the contract and thus becomes unacceptable. For e.g.: selling orange juice in the futures market becomes a Gharar since no one can predict the quality and availability of orange juice in the future.

Gharar also relates to deceit. If a transaction is concluded based on important information being withheld by the seller on purpose, this transaction may be considered invalid under Gharar. For e.g.: if a seller sold a car to a buyer without disclosing there is a major engine problem even though he is aware of it, this may constitute the sale invalid if the seller later discovers the deceit.

Ban on unlawful assets (or products). Any transaction that deals with unlawful products or assets is banned. For e.g.: dealing in arms, tobacco or pork is banned. Likewise, transactions involving gambling industry or prostitution are banned.

Ban on Gambling (Maisir). Gambling and speculation is strictly prohibited under Shariah for the basic reason that gambling or speculation results in uncertainty or Gharar.

What is Islamic Banking?

As we have seen in an earlier section, the foundation for Islamic banking lies in the principles of the Shariah or more specifically on Muamalat, which are based on the Quran and the words and deeds of Prophet Muhammad (called Sunnah or Hadiths).

Under Islamic law all transactions are based on the fundamental tenant that money cannot generate returns unless it is coupled with an activity or work. In other words, money itself has no intrinsic value and therefore people are forbidden from profiting by lending it without accepting a level of risk. Wealth can only be generated via legitimate trade and legitimate investments. And any gain generated must be shared between the person(s) providing the capital and the person(s) providing the expertise.

Thus, any profit should be derived from profit-and-loss and risk-reward sharing arrangements. As such, Shariah law promotes risk sharing between the investor or lender and the user of funds or the borrower. It also encourages the trading of real assets and encourages ownership in the underlying business opportunity.

Also, under Shariah, whatever profits are to be made, they have to be reasonable and provide full visibility to all parties involved. Therefore, extortion or overcharging or taking advantage of other parties is prohibited.

As such, Islamic banking products are strictly based on and reflective of the underlying Shariah contracts. And quite frequently, the products themselves are named based on the underlying names of the contract they employ.

For example: one of the most common Islamic finance products called Murabaha Finance is actually named after an Islamic legal construct called Murabaha and Bai Muajjai. This is a form of credit sale acceptable under Shariah if it meets certain requirements. This is a deferred payment product which allows a buyer to take possession of the goods up front and pay for them later. In conventional finance, banks and even businesses use various names to refer to such sales (e.g.: "Buy now, Pay later"), mostly because there is no specific underlying legal construct these products must conform to other than the specific terms and conditions the borrower is required to sign as long as they don't break any constitutional laws.

Islamic finance is about sharing risks and rewards by all parties involved without any single party bearing excessive risks or rewards. Thus, Islamic finance arrangements must avoid matters that are fundamentally prohibited under Shariah.

The requirement that Islamic finance conform to the principles of Shariah laws is the fundamental difference between conventional banking and Islamic banking. We will discuss more about this in a later section, but for now as a quick intro, the fundamental difference between conventional banking which is practiced in in free-market (capitalistic) economies and Islamic economies is this:

In free market economies business and people are generally free to do what they please. Regulations are enacted to restrain or constrain what people and businesses are allowed to do.

In economics driven by Islamic law, businesses and people are also free to do what they want as long as they conform to Shariah laws. Shariah principles and laws are embedded by default. Regulations are enacted or permissions are given to relax or workaround some of the restraints inherent in the Shariah principles.

Why Islamic Banking?

As mentioned earlier, even though the principles of Islamic finance have been in existence since the religion itself, most conventional banks only started offering Shariah-compliant products around the mid-1970s. More recently, as the oil-fueled economies in the Muslim world became rich and have become major trading partners (UAE, for example), the demand for Islamic (or Shariah compliant) products has seen a significant increase.

In addition, as the indigenous populations in these countries get richer the demand for financing increases for things like automobiles, homes etc. The per capita income in most middle east countries is on par or above most western countries. This demand has also spurred the growth of Shariah compliant products. This demand also made many conventional banks take notice and develop and implement many Shariah compliant finance products.

According to the Global University of Islamic Finance (INCEIF), the global Islamic finance accounts for over $2Trillion in assets and is growing at a double-digit growth (see Global Islamic Banking chart below – Figure 3). Within the past 6 years it more than doubled!

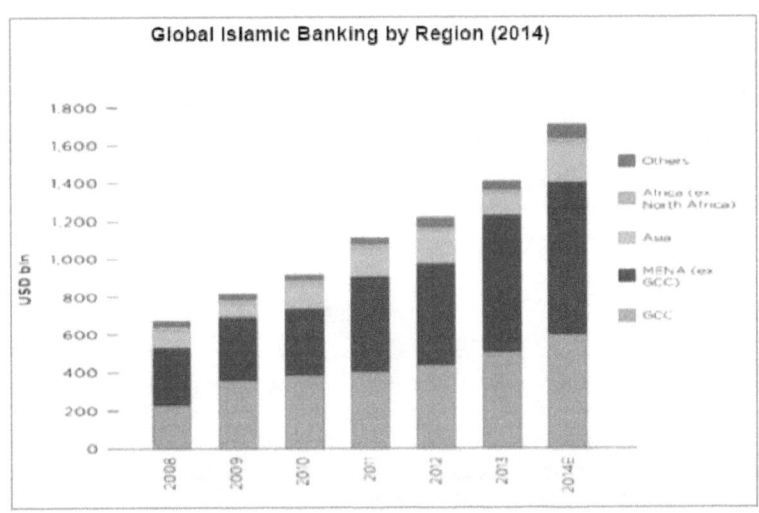

Figure 3 - Source: INCEIF - Global Islamic Banking

Most of this growth is, as expected, in Islamic based countries where Shariah law prevails. However, recently Shariah-compliant capital markets have made inroads into many European countries and other non-Muslim Asian countries. According to the London Telegraph, Chancellor George Osborne is quoted as saying "...the Islamic finance industry, which is worth nearly $2 trillion, would help make Britain "the undisputed centre of the global financial system".

Another fast area of growth is in Islamic Capital Markets related to mostly Islamic bonds called Sukuk. The global Sukuk issuance has grown in excess of USD114Billion in 2014 (see Figure 4 below). For example: according to the London Stock Exchange, "...over US$51 billion has been raised through 57 issues of these alternative finance investment bonds on the London Stock Exchange".

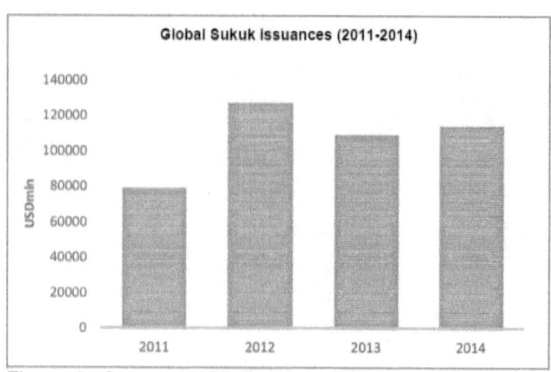

Figure 4 - Source: INCEIF - Global Islamic Capital Market

So, why should you worry about Islamic banking? Because Islamic banking is a growing sector of the global banking industry which is expected to grow double-digits over the next several years. It is a tremendous opportunity for both banks and Corporates to embrace since Islamic finance is based on Shariah laws which provide unique protections that conventional finance does not.

Common Types of Economic Systems

In this chapter we will provide a brief description of the various types of economic systems currently in use or were in use around the world. You are probably well aware of what these are already. However, in order to understand the Islamic economic system and more specifically Islamic Banking, we believe providing a brief background is essential since one of the objectives of this book is to compare conventional banking to Islamic banking.

Generally, there are five common types of economies:
- ⬚ Free Market Economies
- ⬚ Command Economies
- ⬚ Mixed Economies
- ⬚ Traditional Economies
- ⬚ Islamic Economies

Free Market (Capitalistic) Economies.

A free market economy, also known as "hands off" or laissez-faire economies, completely relies on the market to solve the economic problems. The government usually does not get involved and there are very few regulations in a truly free market economy. In this model, consumers determine what to produce and producers determine how to produce. Who buys the products depends upon who can afford it.

General features of Free Market / Capitalist Economic System

• The government generally does not play a role in economic activity.

• Generally, there are very few regulations with emphasis on freedom of the individuals (consumers and producers).

• The private sector owns most of the industries and businesses.

• Profit maximization is the main goal in this economy.

• The supply and demand and competition determine the price.

Advantages

• Manufacturers are free to produce what the consumers want and the consumers in turn are free to spend their money as they see fit.

• The decision of what to produce is not controlled by the government or any single individual/firm. Hence, there is greater innovation and diversity in products produced.

• The supply and demand and competition determine the price.

• There is freedom from government interference.

• Profit motive encourages efficiency in production.

- Competition among firms improves quality, keeps prices low and spurs new technology and innovation.

Disadvantages:

- Since profit is the dominant motive of the private sector, only goods and services that yield the highest profit are produced.

- Individual choice generally means individual benefits rule over the benefits to society.

- Since there are no regulations, consumers could be exploited through the charging of high prices for essential goods and services.

- This system may lead to great inequalities as the rich get richer and the poor get poorer.

- Lack of regulation may lead to pollution (smog and chemical and oil leaks).

- May lead to increased production of what society may consider sinful goods such as alcohol, cigarettes and illegal drugs.

Example of Free Market Economies:
Currently there are no real life examples of a purely free market economy as most countries implement some government regulation. A pure free market system only exists in theory.

Command or Planned or Socialistic Economies
Command economic system is where the government, rather than the free market, determines what goods should be produced, how much they should be produced and at what price the goods should be sold.

General features of Command or Planned Economic System

- State controls all economic activity

- State makes all decisions regarding economic activities

- State decides what goods are produced, how much of each good to produce and how much the people should get (people lining up to get bread in the former Soviet Union is a good example)

Advantages

- Emphasizes society benefits over individuals - the welfare of all citizens is the main goal.

- Generally, there is very low unemployment since the government is the primary employer; the government sets the wages.

- Government can direct resources where they are most needed.

- Wasteful competition is avoided.

- There are no labor strikes.

- Greater emphasis on quality of life rather than on quantity produced.

Disadvantages

- No freedom of choice for consumers or producers.

- In reality, welfare of all citizens is often not realized; most of the wealth is accumulated with the people in power.

- Corruption is rampant.

- Lack of incentive for workers results in low morale and low motivation resulting in inefficiency and lower productivity.

- Lack of profit incentive for producers results in lack of innovation and lack of competition and lower quality of products and services.

- There is too much red-tape or bureaucracy.

- Conflicts of interests can arise because what the country needs may not be what the people want.

Example of Command Economies:
The former Soviet Union, North Korea and China (until recently).

Mixed (Market) Economies.
A mixed economic system is a combination of free market economy and command economy. Mixed economies generally have a private sector (like the

free market) where the market usually determines what is produced and by whom and at what cost. But mixed economies also have a distinct public sector, where the government makes some decisions. For e.g.: the government may make decisions related to national defense, national healthcare, police and fire services. However, generally, since the government is democratically elected by the people, the decisions made by the government are considered to be indirectly made by the people themselves.

In addition, in mixed economies the government may also pass regulations which control how consumers and producers may behave. For e.g.: regulations related to industrial waste by companies or regulation related to how much water or power people may consume (where water and power shortages are severe) may be set by the government. For example: in California, some cities have severe restrictions on water usage due to drought conditions.

There is a wide variation on the mixed economies with some economies leaning more to the free market side (e.g.: USA) to some economics leaning more towards Command economies (e.g.: China). See Figure 5 below.

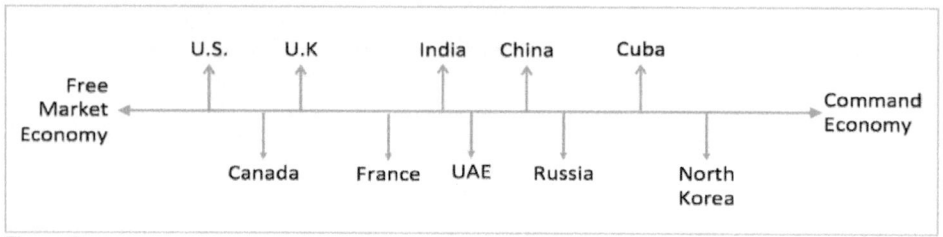

Figure 5

Traditional Economies

An economic system in which traditions, customs, and beliefs shape the goods and the services the economy produces, as well as the rules and manner of their distribution. Countries that use this type of economic system are often rural and generally rely on hunting, fishing and farm-based economies. Large-scale industries do not exist nor does a well-defined legal and regulatory system.

General features of Traditional Economic System:

• Existence is primarily based on traditions and customs.

• Bartering is the main form of trading.

• Individuals survive at subsistence level.

26

- The decision of what to produce and how much and for whom is determined by customs and traditions.

- Resources were owned or controlled by a sovereign or feudal lord.

Advantages:

- Members of the society know exactly what they are to do.

- There is a community spirit.

- Hierarchy within society is well established.

- Economic issues are dealt with by traditions and customs.

- Life is generally stable, predictable and continuous.

Disadvantages:

- This type of society is often very slow to change.

- Significantly lacks in technological, intellectual and scientific development.

- Is very inefficient as there is no specialization or industrial scale.

- Reliance on natural forces (rain etc) leads to periods of low production of food.

- No upward movement of labor forces.
- Society is generally considered backwards and with basic subsistence.

Examples of this economic system:
- Remote tribal areas in South America, Africa and Asia

Islamic Economies.
Islamic economies come in two flavors. They are based entirely on Shariah law. Or they allow mixed-markets and Shariah compliant economic systems to co-exist thus becoming "hybrid" economies that prohibit interest but allow socially responsible investments.

Most Islamic countries currently fall under hybrid economies.

Mixed (Market) Economies v/s Islamic Economies

As we mentioned in the previous chapter, truly free market economies really do not exist. What is commonly found are mixed economies. Mixed economies are a hybrid of free market capitalism and controlled economies. These are also known as market economies where there is a strong government oversight with free market elements in play.

There is a wide variation in the mixed economies. Mixed economies in some countries lean more towards a free market and less controlled (eg: USA, UK etc) whereas in other countries they lean more towards controlled economy and less free market (Italy, Mexico). In this chapter we will compare the differences between mixed economies and Islamic economies. However, in order to provide a better context, let's take a brief look at the history of capitalism which is what mixed market economies are based on.

A brief history of modern capitalism

Modern capitalism is based on the ideas of Adam Smith and John Keynes. Adam Smith believed in division of labor (specialization) and the almost limitless possibilities for society to expand its wealth through manufacture and trade. He also believed in the limited economic power of government. This idea gave rise to the industrial revolution and mechanical power in the 18th and 19th centuries, which transformed civilization. Mechanical power brought an increase in worker efficiency, which made goods cheap and abundantly available. This also gave rise to the modern working class where workers no longer had to own their tools as the tools were provided in the factories. They had little property and had to exchange their labor for wages.

However, the industrial revolution had a serious human cost. In the early days of the Industrial Revolution appalling conditions for large numbers of workers was commonplace. Child labor, long working hours and dangerous and unhealthy workplaces were commonplace. The industrial revolution also led to dominance of businesses leading to monopolies. The public outcry about such conditions gave rise to regulations. For example: in the U.S., antitrust legislation was enacted by Congress in 1915 to restrict such monopolistic practices and to bring about more competition into the marketplace. Another legacy of the industrial revolution was the boom-and-bust cycles of expansion and prosperity followed by economic collapse and high unemployment.

Towards the mid 20th century, John Keynes, on the other hand demonstrated that the government has a role to play in managing economic growth by using its power to spend money, vary taxes and control the money supply. According to Keynes, if an economy is going into recession or depression, the government should increase its spending to offset the decline in private spending even at the cost of unbalanced budgets. This process could be reversed if a boom leads to excessive speculation and inflation. He believed that the governments should kick-start the economies when needed and restrain spending when the economies run wild. Doing this should allow the governments to control the recessions and inflation cycles better and allow economies to grow at a reasonable pace. Most western economics subscribe to a hybrid Adam Smith and Keynes's economic model, especially the U.S. and U.K. This hybrid model allows these economies to operate as market economies in that they keep the government out of economic activities but also allow the government to get involved in spending or restricting the money flow (by limiting government spending or raising interest rates) as needed.

However, the philosophy of limited role of government in business led to excess speculation that led to the financial market collapse that in turn led to the Depression in 1929. To curb such excess speculation, governments began to intervene in the economy to correct the worst abuses inherent in capitalism. For e.g.: in the U.S., the administration of President Franklin D. Roosevelt restructured the financial system to prevent the repeat of the speculative excesses that had led to financial collapse in 1929. Collective bargaining and a strong labor movement was also encouraged in order to offset the concentration of economic power in large industrial corporations.

In addition, in the US, social security and unemployment benefits were introduced which were measures designed to protect people from the economic hazards endemic to a capitalist system. Social security and unemployment form the foundation of the modern welfare system in the U.S.

For a couple of decades after World War II, free market capitalism proved extraordinarily successful. Western capitalist countries enjoyed nearly uninterrupted and unprecedented growth, low rates of inflation, and ever-increasing living standards.

Cracks in Capitalism

Beginning in the late 1960s, however, due to various reasons, the boom and bust cycles began to repeat and repeat more frequently. The recent recessions in the year 1997 (Asian financial crisis) followed by recession in 2000 (dot com bubble), followed by 2007/2008 (subprime mortgage) are good examples of the boom and bust cycles. The world has never fully recovered from the 2008 financial meltdown. There were many other recessions in between the ones listed above which had significant regional impact. And these recessions seem to be occurring more and more frequently.

All of these recessions can be traced to some uncontrolled excess due to lack of (or lenient) regulations. For e.g.: the recession in 2000 was a result of speculation in the stock market that led to incredible valuations of technology stock prices even though the underlying value of the companies was nowhere close. All of this came tumbling down when the companies failed to deliver expected results.

The more recent 2007/2008 subprime mortgage crisis in the US involved and impacted the major economies of the world. Subprime mortgages and derivatives of these subprime mortgages were packaged into mortgage backed securities and called Collateral Debt Obligations (CDO) and sold and resold as high quality "AAA" securities to commercial banks and investment banks, large investors and even countries looking for higher return on investments. However, with the decline of the real estate market especially in markets like California and Florida where the market has seen significant growth, these securities became worthless. This in turn resulted in historic losses at the largest banks around the world, which in turn caused collateral damage to other banks that dealt with these banks. Most banks were connected deeply with these securities and if one failed there was a real risk that it would cause a domino effect and take out other banks. This would have resulted in a complete collapse of the entire financial markets.

Therefore, governments in the US and UK and other countries had to step in and provide over $1.5 Trillion in rescue packages to some banks. The US government "bailed out" Freddie Mac and Fannie May, both of which are institutions providing guarantees for mortgage loans.

In addition, AIG, which was the largest insurance company in the US, was on the verge of collapse and had to be rescued by the US government. Why an insurance company? Because the banks and investment companies who bought the mortgage backed securities also bought Credit Default Swaps (CDS), which are basically insurance policies against the mortgages. And AIG sold CDSs worth billions of dollars. In fact, it was estimated that the CDS market in 2007 was at $60 trillion (Reuters: The Big Money: How AIG fell apart). Banks, hedge funds and insurance companies were buying and selling the CDS without actually buying the underlying securities. And as these mortgage-backed securities began to fail, the insurance claims became due, and AIG did not have the money to cover all the claims. The fact that these securities were backed up with insurance policies (CDS), allowed the ratings agencies to assign them with the highest "AAA" credit ratings.

A brief detour to see why the Subprime crisis happened (you may skip this section if you like).

So, why and how did this financial crisis happen?

Four main reasons:
• Low interest rates.
• Careless or even fraudulent mortgage lending practices and the belief that home prices will always go up.
• Creation of new mortgage loan products and securitization of such mortgages.
• Lack of regulations or lack of enforcement of the regulations.

For well over 2 decades now, the interest rates in the US and most of the western world remained low. One could get mortgage loans as low as 1% or 2% interest rates. These low rates came about as the governments pushed the interest rates down as a way to boost the economies to get out of recessions.

However, this prolonged low interest rates had a very negative impact on large and institutional investors who typically invest in very secure, very liquid "AAA" rated investments such as US Treasury Bills or corporate bonds. Because such investments were paying very little interest, these investors began looking for alternative sources of investments that provided better returns. They discovered mortgage-backed securities.

In the beginning, the mortgage backed securities were safe as the mortgage companies who provided the loans were very careful and conducted proper due diligence to ensure the borrowers were capable of making the mortgage payments before lending them money. This was mostly because the lenders were taking a significant risk by making these loans. However, as the demand for mortgage-backed securities heated up, the mortgage lenders (or originators) found themselves as middlemen; they were originating the loans which were immediately bought by banks and investment banks who then securitized these loans and sold them to other investors. Soon, the mortgage lenders found themselves with no skin in the game (i.e.: they did not take any risk). They became factories churning the mortgages that were immediately sold. They made their money from the fees they were charging the borrowers. The bankers and investment banks that bought these mortgages from the originators packaged them into other mortgage-backed securities and sold them off to others. And in cases where they kept these loans on their books, they took out insurance policies against them (Credit Default Swaps) mitigating the risk of default. As these mortgages were originating and sold and resold, each person along the way earned a huge amount of fees. And since they did not hold on to any of these mortgages, they were not taking any risks. Soon the name of the game was to churn as many mortgages as possible to make as much in fees as possible. Inevitably, the lending practices went lax. The originators did not care if the borrower was capable of paying the mortgages; all they had to do was provide loans to anyone and turn around and sell them. And there was no shortage of borrowers and buyers.

Adding to this euphoria was the fact that the home prices kept going up and up. This was mostly driven by the fact that since interest rates were low, more people were qualified to buy the homes as they could afford lower mortgage payments. On top of this, mortgage lenders came up with clever mortgage products to attract even more buyers. Products such as, ARM loans (adjustable rate mortgages), Interest Only Loans, Minimal Documents/No Documents loans, NINJA (no income, no job application) loans, negative amortization loans and subprime loans. All of these were designed to get more people to "qualify" to buy homes; it did not matter if they actually had income to pay these mortgages or not. Mortgage originators were making huge amounts of money just by originating the loans and selling them.

A lot of buyers bought these exotic mortgage products fully knowing they could not afford the homes they were buying simply because they thought they could sell the homes in a few months and make a lot of money. Why? Because everyone thought the home prices would continue to go up, and indeed, in the beginning they were. In fact things got so crazy that it was not unusual to see bidding wars to purchase homes. Sometimes the sellers were getting offers that were 20% to 30% more than their asking prices! Many sellers put their homes on the market without an asking price and inviting bidders (basically auctioning them).

As the home prices inevitably started to come down, the people who bought the homes using some of the exotic mortgage products could not continue to pay the mortgages or sell their homes quickly to get out of debt. Worse, some of these mortgages, like interest only loans or negative amortization loans, added to the original amount borrowed. And since home prices were going down, a lot of buyers found that what they "owed" on the mortgage was more than the home was worth. This was called being "under-water". Because of this, many homebuyers simply walked away from their homes. This caused a snowball effect and as the home prices tumbled, the mortgage defaults rose and soon the investors who held the insurance policies were calling on the policies and insurance companies like AIG and other banks and investments firms quickly found that they could not honor these insurance policies. This in turn created a "systemic risk" in that if one bank or investment firm failed, the insurance policies they issued would not be honored which in turn could cause other investors who held these policies to fail and so on.

The regulators who were supposed to regulate the mortgage loans and especially the securitization of mortgages were asleep at the switch. The rating agencies who gave the CDOs "AAA" ratings did not do the due diligence they should have done. And the investors who bought these securities did not do their job to ensure what they were buying were solid investments. And finally, the borrowers who took out the loans either did not understand what they were getting into or were under the impression that they could sell their homes quickly and make a lot of profit. There was euphoria everywhere in the beginning; when the cards came tumbling down, the euphoria led to panic and things got into a crisis.

Fortunately, the measures taken by governments succeeded and a catastrophic collapse of the global financial markets was avoided. However, even to this day, most of the world is still reeling from this mess and things have not fully recovered yet.

We have provided a more detailed explanation of what happened during the 2008 financial market mess because of two reasons. One, since this happened not so long ago, you probably still remember it and easily relate to it and two, to provide proof that once again the excess and lack of proper regulation typical in a mixed market economy, led to this fiasco.

If the markets are left to do whatever they want in a mixed-market economy, sometimes things go crazy because maximization of profits always takes precedence over what's good for the society.

After this recession, many countries implemented stricter regulations to curb such excess in the future. For example, in the USA, Dodd–Frank Wall Street Reform and Consumer Protection Act was enacted in 2010 which included new laws related to mortgage loan disclosures, regulations on lending practices, regulations on short selling etc. Similarly, such regulations were adopted in the UK and other countries.

In fact, one of the provisions under the Consumer Protection Act of 2010 was the following requirement:

Skin in the Game: Requires companies that sell products like mortgage backed securities to retain at least 5% of the credit risk, unless the underlying loans meet standards that reduce riskiness. That way if the investment doesn't pan out, the company that packaged and sold the investment would lose out right along with the people they sold it to.

If one goes back and looks at what happened after the previous recessions a common theme emerges. After every recession, there is usually a flurry of activity to pass new regulations to curb the excesses that caused the recession in the first place. And this generally occurs after every recession. The main reason behind is this. The governments in the free-market economies have limited power. It is believed that the free enterprise and market forces will naturally govern themselves and enforce checks and balances. So, when excess of any form occurs and they lead to recessions or other financial catastrophes, regulations are enacted to curb such excesses. And during boom time, the regulations previously enacted get thrown out which in turn leads to more excesses and eventually to another downturn.

Would the Subprime crisis have occurred under Islamic system?

It is said that in a capitalistic system, sometimes for someone to win, someone else has to lose; for someone to succeed, someone else has to fail. Indeed, in the subprime crisis, there were many who won in the beginning as the home prices were going up. But a lot more people lost at the end.

This is very different in Islamic system. _Because of the requirement that profits and risks must be shared, one does not have to lose for someone else to win and one does not have to fail for someone else to succeed._ Under Shariah, the profits must be just and the gains and losses must be shared. So, all the parties to a transaction succeed or all of them lose; it's win-win or lose-lose.

Under Islamic finance, the speculative practices of Collateral Debt Obligations and Credit Default Swaps would not have been allowed. This is because under these instruments there is no underlying asset that one owns. Shariah law requires that an underlying real asset must be owned for it to be sold.

Likewise, the fraudulent lending practices and the exotic mortgage products that contributed to the subprime crisis would not have been allowed in Islamic finance. This is because there is significant uncertainty (Gharar) in such products. For e.g.: on Adjustable-rate mortgages (ARMs) the interest rate is variable and therefore is uncertain – not allowed under Shariah. Likewise, NINJA (no income no job) type of loans would not be allowed since Islamic finance requires the lender to perform more due diligence and require more transparency. Thus, practices such as no income loans, no documentation loans, no down payment loans etc. would have been very visible to buyers of these mortgages.

Shariah looks at money not as something that can be rented at a price (the interest rate), but as a tool to help with the success or failure of investing. Shariah is also concerned with the type of investment in which money is invested. Thus, investing in speculative instruments would have been prohibited.

So, here's the main point.
The free market or mixed market systems are based on limited regulation initially and only pass regulation as needed to curb excesses. This is because mixed economies are secular in nature. That is, there is a separation between the legal construct and religion. Therefore, the requirements or guidelines present in religion are not intrinsically part of the legal system that governs business transactions. Since government interference is limited in mixed economies, regulations must be passed to limit what people and corporations can do.

In Shariah compliant economies there is no separation between the legal construct and the religion since under Islam, religion and the way of life are intertwined. Therefore, the Shariah principles are intrinsically part of the legal system that governs business transactions. Everyone is required to conform to the Shariah principles in business transactions by default. Regulations or permissions are given by the Shariah Supervisory Boards (more on this later) subject to interpretations to relax or workaround some of the limits imposed by Shariah.

This distinction is very important so we will state it again.

Islamic banking is based on Shariah law. Shariah law is part of the Quran, which contains the fundamental tenets of Islamic religion. Therefore, the principles of Islamic banking, which we have seen earlier, are by default derived from Islamic religion. Thus, unlike what we have seen in mixed market economics, regulations are not needed to enforce these principles; they are part and parcel of the way of life of the people who believe in Islam.

So the bottom line is this. If Islamic finance products follow the strict principles of Shariah law, permission or approval is not needed. If they deviate slightly or if there is a question whether or not they conform to Shariah law, approval from the Shariah Supervisor Board must be sought.

Therefore, approvals from the Shariah Supervisor Board act as permission to do something where its conformity with Shariah is not clear or is subject to interpretation.

Whereas in mixed-market economics, the people and business are free to do whatever they want. The regulations are passed to limit one from doing certain things (i.e.: take something away).

This is the fundamental difference between mixed market economic systems (capitalism) and Islamic economic systems.

By the way, as an aside, it is interesting to note that even in Christianity, charging interest is also prohibited. For instance, in Exodus and Deuteronomy it is mentioned that charging interest is not acceptable:

> Exodus 22:25: "If you lend money to any of my people with you who is poor, you shall not be like a moneylender to him, and you shall not exact interest from him".

Deuteronomy 23:19: "You shall not charge interest on loans to your brother, interest on money, interest on food, interest on anything that is lent for interest".

Due to the fact that free market societies are secular in nature and separation of state and religion is part of the constitution and belief systems, the religious beliefs and requirements do not automatically become part of the legal requirements that govern business transactions. Therefore, regulations may need to be enacted to enforce practices even though these practices may already be part of the religion that may predominate in such countries.

Common Islamic Contracts

As we discussed in the previous chapter, Islamic banking products are based on specific types of underlying contracts. These Shariah-compliant contracts support productive economic activities while adhering to key Islamic principles. For e.g.:, Shariah compliant contracts cannot create debt, cannot involve the payment of interest, and must provide for a sharing of risk and responsibility between the involved parties.

To be valid, an Islamic contract must be lawful and be specific enough to avoid uncertainties. Additionally, the service or asset described in the contract generally must exist when the contract is being created and must be owned by the seller and must be deliverable. If any uncertainty is present about its compliance with Shariah, concurrence from the Shariah Compliance Board must be sought. Some of the commonly used contracts in Islamic finance are:

Contracts of partnership – these allow two or more parties to form partnerships in order to develop and grow commercial enterprises by sharing both risk and return.

Mudaraba: One party gives money to another party (known as the fund manager), who invests it in a business or economic activity. Both parties share any profit made from the investment (based on a pre-agreed ratio), but only the investor loses money if the investment flops. The fund manager loses the value of the time and effort they dedicated to the investment. However, the fund manager assumes financial responsibility if the loss results from their negligence.

Musharaka: This contract creates a joint venture in which both parties provide investment capital, entrepreneurial skills, and labor and both share the profit and/or loss of the activity.

Contracts of exchange are sales contracts that allow for the transfer of a commodity for another commodity or the transfer of a commodity for money or the transfer of money for money:

Murabaha: this is a cost-plus contract, where a seller sells a commodity to a buyer disclosing its cost and the profit margin wherein both parties know the cost and the profit in advance. The buyer may make the payment in lump sum or make deferred payments.

Bai Salam: this is a forward contract, where the buyer (or an Islamic financial institution on behalf of the buyer) pays for goods in full in advance, and the goods are delivered in the future.

Istisna: a variant of the forward contract, in an Istisna contract, an Islamic financial institution will buy a asset, on behalf of the buyer, that is under construction and will be completed and delivered on a future date.

Wadiah: An individual or corporation gives money or property to another party for the purpose of safeguarding. In Islamic banks, current (checking) accounts and savings accounts, where the bank's customers deposit money into these accounts, are based on the Wadiah contract. Money deposited into these accounts are safeguarded by the banks and generally the customers do not get anything in return other than access to their funds whenever they need it.

Hiwala: under this contract, a debtor assigns the debt to a third party with the approval from the lender. After the debt is transferred to the third party, the original debtor is freed from their obligation. The third party continues to pay the installment amount to the lender until the debt is paid off. This option is typically used by debtors (borrowers) to avoid going through litigation if they find themselves unable to pay monthly installments. The third party who has assumed the debt usually does so because they may be getting a better deal. For eg: if the debtor is unable to make house payments, he/she may decide to assign (or transfer) their house to a third party at below market value who then assumes the responsibility and continues to pay the lender. This also provides the benefit to the third party of avoiding the process of applying, qualifying and getting a loan in their name if they were to buy this property. By taking over the property and the assignment of the debt, the third party thus benefits (assuming the lender agrees to this). This is similar to assignment of loan under conventional banking.

Kafala: is used by the banks to provide guarantee services, such as bank guarantee, standby letter of credit and shipping guarantees. This is where a third party accepts an existing obligation and becomes responsible for fulfilling someone's liability. We will discuss this more under financing under Trade later in this book.

Rahn: under this contract, a property is pledged as a collateral for a loan. A customer of the bank may offer a collateral or a pledge via a Rahn contract in order to secure a loan or a Letter of Credit (to be discussed later).

The above-mentioned contracts in order to be enforced must have the contracts drawn and completed. Contracts that involve prohibited items or contracts that are structured in a way that do not conform to Shariah may result in the entire contract being nullified.

Basic Rules of a Valid Sale

Before we look at the common Islamic Banking products, we will take a look at some of the basic rules of a valid sale.

Basic Rules of a Valid Sale
Under Shariah law, a "sale" is defined as transfer of something in exchange for something of equal value. A sale contract could be in written form, or in verbal form (eg.: if a Buyer says "I want to buy 1 dozen eggs for $2" and if the Seller agrees, it is a valid sale). A sale may also be implied by some action. For eg: a buyer goes into a candy store and picks up a candy bar which has the price marked on it and pays for it and leaves the store without any verbal exchange. Since the seller clearly marked the sale price and the buyer implicitly agreed to the price by paying for it, it constitutes a valid sale.

A sale must also adhere to the following rules (according to religious scholar Maulana Taqi Usmani):

Rule 1: The subject of sale must exist at the time of sale.
Thus, a thing that has not yet come into existence cannot be sold. If a non-existent thing has been sold the sale is considered void according to Shariah even if both parties mutually agree to it. Example: a seller sells an unborn camel to a buyer. The sale is void as there is uncertainty over if the unborn camel would be born alive or not and this uncertainty in a sale is not allowed under Shariah. Exceptions are Bay Salam and Istisna contracts which are discussed later in this book.

Rule 2: The seller must own the subject of sale at the time of sale.
Something that is not owned by the seller cannot be sold. If a seller sells something before owning it, the sale is considered void. Example: A sells to B

shares in a company which he intends to buy in the future (short selling). This sale is void, because A does not own the shares at the time of sales agreement (with the exception of Bay Salam and Istisna contracts).

Rule 3: As an extension to the above rule, the subject of sale must be in the physical or constructive possession of the seller when the seller sells it to another person.

"Constructive possession" means even if the seller has not taken physical delivery of the commodity, the commodity has come into the seller's control, and all the rights and liabilities of the commodity are passed on to the seller, including the risk of its destruction. For example, A has purchased a car from B but B has not yet delivered it to A. However, if the title is transferred and money exchanged, the risk may be considered as passed to A. The car in this case is considered to be in constructive possession of A. If A sells the car to someone else even without acquiring physical possession, the sale is valid because A has had constructive possession.

The gist of the 3 rules mentioned above is that a seller cannot sell a commodity unless:
a. It has come into existence.
b. It is actually owned by the seller.
c. It is in the physical or constructive possession of the seller.

Exceptions being Bay Salam and Istisna contracts.

These rules are important to remember, as they become the basis for some of the Islamic financing products we will encounter in later chapters.

There are some exceptions to these rules. First is that a promise to sell something that is not yet owned or possessed creates only a moral obligation and is not a valid sale contract. For e.g.: an airline manufacturer promises to sell an aircraft to an airline company even though it has not yet been built. In this case, if the airline manufacturer does not meet its promise, the airline company may lose revenue since it cannot fly the plane. In such cases a contract type called Istisna is utilized. Thing to note is that, a separate sales contract must be executed when the time comes to buy the commodity that the seller promised to deliver in the future. The promise itself is not a sales contract.

The other exception is "Bai Salam" where the buyer pays in advance for the sale but the delivery of the goods is deferred in the future.

Rule 4: The sale must be instant and absolute.

A sale that is contingent upon something or a sale to occur in the future (with the exception of Istisna as discussed above) is not a valid sale. For example:

1. A says to B on the first of January: "I will sell my car to you on the first of February". The sale is considered invalid, because it is effective at a future date and there is uncertainty. The car may get stolen or break down etc.

2. A says to B, "If my team wins the game, I will buy your car". The sale is void, because it is contingent on a future and uncertain event.

Rule 5: The subject of sale must be something of value.

Rule 6: The subject of sale should not be a prohibited item in Shariah such as pork, wine, tobacco etc.

Rule 7: The subject of sale must be identified specifically to the buyer.
The subject of sale may be identified either by gesture or by detailed specification that can distinguish it from other things not sold. For example:

Let's say, one goes to a car dealer to buy a car. In the lot there are several cars that are the same model with same specifications and price. The dealer says to a buyer, "I will sell you one of these cars" and the buyer accepts. The sale is void because the specific car which was intended to be sold to the buyer had not been identified or pointed out.

Rule 8: The delivery of the sold commodity to the buyer must be certain and should not depend on a contingency or chance.

For example: A sells his crop to B at a low price only if there is plenty of rainfall in the future resulting in a bountiful harvest. The sale is void as there is uncertainty (Gharar).

Rule 9: The certainty of price is a necessary condition for the validity of a sale. If the price is uncertain, the sale is void. For example:

A says to B, "If you pay within a month, the price is $50. If you pay after two months, the price will be $55". B agrees. Since the final price is uncertain the sale is void unless both A and B agree to one price or the other upfront.

Rule 10: The sale must be unconditional. A conditional sale is invalid, unless the condition is recognized as a part of the transaction according to the usage of trade. For example:

1. A buys a car from B on a condition that B will provide A access to his vacation home for a week. The sale is invalid since this condition is not considered "normal" for this type of sale.

2. A buys a refrigerator from B, with a condition that B includes repairs for 2 years. The condition, being recognized as a part of the transaction, is valid and the sale is lawful.

It is important to remember these rules as they apply to Islamic banking products which we will look at next.

Common Islamic Banking Products

The common types of Islamic banking products are shown below (Figure 6 below). Since the objectives of this book are focused on Islamic Corporate Transaction Banking products we will only focus on these topics below.

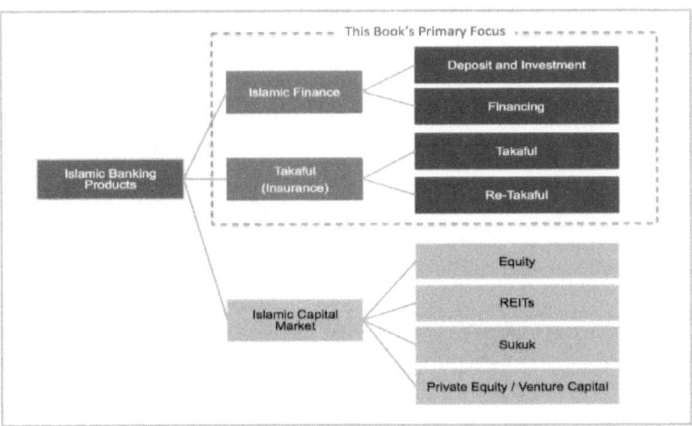

Figure 6

Deposits and Investments products relate to where the customer is depositing or investing their funds with a bank to earn interest or profit in conventional banking. Under Islamic finance these products work slightly differently since interest is not allowed.   The following (Figure 7) is a breakdown of Islamic deposit and investment products.

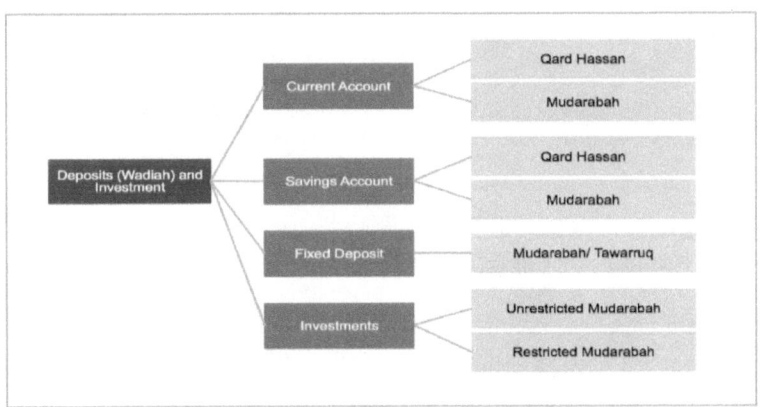

Figure 7

Deposit or Wadiah Accounts

In Arabic, Wadiah means deposit. These are therefore accounts that can be saving or checking or fixed deposit accounts.

Current (or checking) Accounts

Qard Hassan Checking Account - This account is based on the Islamic principle of "Qard Hassan", which is considered an interest free loan. In this case, the depositor is giving the bank money without expecting anything in return. The bank is basically "safeguarding" the depositor's money and is required to return the amount left in the account any time upon request from the depositor. The bank may offer services like check books or money transfers from this account. Depending on the minimum amount held in the account the bank may waive the charges for such services. This is very similar to conventional banking checking accounts that corporations hold with banks.

Mudaraba Checking Account – this type of account is offered in cases where the bank offers a return on the checking account. The depositor is called "arbab al mal" and the bank that plays the role of fund manager or working partner is called "mudarib". In conventional banking, the bank may offer interest on the available balance in the checking account. In Islamic banking sense, the bank is required to invest the funds according to Shariah guidelines and offers a "profit" to the depositor or investor. The profit is shared between the bank and the depositor and both parties agree upfront on how the profits are split between them. Any losses, however, are solely borne by the depositor. The important difference between this account and a conventional account is that the customers' funds are invested by the bank in Shariah compliant Islamic assets. Any losses are borne by the depositor alone. The bank's skin-in-the-game is the loss of time and effort by the bank in investing the depositors money. In conventional banking, the depositor becomes a creditor to the bank and the bank must pay the depositor even if it makes a loss. In cases where the bank declares bankruptcy or goes under, different rules apply.

Savings Accounts

Qard Hassan Saving Accounts and Mudaraba Saving Account work similar to checking accounts described above with the exception that the accounts themselves offer different features. For e.g.: checking accounts may offer check books and debit cards and expect frequent deposits and withdrawals whereas savings accounts offer limited features.

Profit v/s Interest?

By now you may be wondering what is the difference if the depositor is getting a profit or is getting paid an interest since both interest and profit are generally quoted as a percent return per annum? In Islamic banking the bank may say it will pay you 2.3% profit on your deposit. Whereas in conventional banking the bank may say it will pay you 2.3% interest on your deposit. So, what is the difference?

The difference is this: in conventional banking, if the bank says it will pay 2.3% interest, it is obligated to pay 2.3% interest no matter if the bank made money or not on the money you deposited. Banks generally use the depositor's money to make loans to other customers at a higher interest rate or make investments and earn more than they are paying the depositor. Under conventional banking, the bank has to pay the interest to its depositors regardless if it makes money or not. Under Islamic banking, the bank is only obligated to pay if it makes money from the investments it made using your money. If the bank makes a bad investment with the depositor's money and incurs a loss, the depositor either shares the loss or bears the full loss. The bank is under no obligation to pay the depositor any profit. Now that is a significant difference!

Fixed Deposits

Mudaraba Fixed Deposit – works similar to the Mudaraba saving account except that the term of the deposit is in fixed increments and the depositor cannot withdraw the money before the term expires. In some cases, the depositor may be allowed to withdraw early but incurring a penalty.

Tawarruq Fixed Deposit – this is a more complex form of deposit product as it uses two contract types to achieve its objective. This deposit type is used to offer guaranteed profit to depositors. In this product, Murabaha (cost plus profit) contract and Tawarruq contract are employed.

Generally, the only way an Islamic bank can accept cash deposit is by using Mudaraba deposit where the profits or losses have to be shared with the depositor (as discussed before). Any offer of a guaranteed profit is not allowed as it goes against Shariah principles (cannot earn money on money). So, how does a bank offer guaranteed profits? The banks do it by combining multiple sales and purchase contracts.

In the first contract, the buyer purchases a commodity on a deferred payment basis (using Bai Muajjal sale which is covered later in this book) from the seller, and the second contract involves the buyer selling the same commodity to a third party on a spot payment basis (meaning that payment is made on the spot).

Thus, the buyer on one hand, by buying the commodity on a deferred payment basis owns the commodity (without paying for it) and by immediately selling the commodity on a spot payment basis gets the cash they want. They then pay the seller on a deferred payment basis. The buyer in this case is the Bank (as they are paying guaranteed profits to the depositor) and the depositor is the seller (the one paying for the commodity).

It works as follows:

- Step1, the bank, or typically its subsidiary acting as a Purchasing agent for the customer, purchases commodities using money from the customer (the deposit) by paying cash on a spot basis. Let's say the cost is $100,000. The customer (depositor) owns the commodity.

- Step2, the bank, or its subsidiary, now acting as a Sales agent for the customer (under a new relationship) sells this commodity to the bank for cost plus profit on a deferred payment basis. In this case the profit component of the cost-plus profit contract is the guaranteed amount the bank offers which is paid in installments to the customer by the bank.

- Step3, the bank then immediately sells the commodity to a third party for cash on a spot basis. So, the bank gets its money back minus the profit component.

- Step4, the bank pays the customer agreed upon guaranteed profits on an installment basis as deferred payments.

At the end of this, essentially, the money from the customer makes it to the bank and the bank agrees to pay the customer the guaranteed amount as the interest (or profit) they would have normally earned. Except, this time, it is workaround as a deferred payment from the sale. Let's take a look at how this conforms to Shariah law.

In Step1, the Customer using the bank's subsidiary as a Purchasing agent of the customer purchases commodity for cash on spot basis in a straight forward Mudaraba contract. Customer is the owner of the commodity. So, instead of giving the money to the bank for deposit, the customer buys a commodity.

In Step2, the Customer, now using the bank's subsidiary as a sales agent, sells the commodity to the bank for cost plus profit using Murabaha contract where the cost and project margin is disclosed up front and payable as deferred payment. Customers can do this as they legally own the commodity. Bank now owns the commodity but agrees to pay the Customer at a later date. The cost component of the "cost plus profit" sale is the deposit amount; the "plus profit" component of the sale is the installment amount which is the fixed profit which is paid in installments (same as interest in a conventional sense).

Note that the bank still does not have the money yet. The bank gets access to the money in the next step.

In Step3, the bank which now owns the commodity, sells it to a third party for cash on a spot sale. Bank now has access to the money (similar to a customer giving money to the bank to open a deposit account).

In Step4, the bank makes the agreed upon profit in installment payments to the Customer.

In conventional fixed deposits, the customer opens a fixed deposit account by giving the money to the bank and the bank pays a fixed rate of interest. However, under Islamic finance, the bank cannot offer a fixed rate of profit for money as it does not know what the future returns on its investments will bring. If you recall from previous discussions, under Shariah law, the bank and the customer must share in the profits the bank makes on the money deposited (invested) by its customer. Since the bank cannot predict the future profits, it cannot provide a guaranteed profit. Therefore, the bank has to use the steps mentioned above to make this transaction legit under Shariah.

The difference between Tawarruq fixed deposit and the Mudaraba fixed deposit (described above) is that under Tawarruq, the loss is not passed on to the depositor. This is because, in step 2 above where the cost-plus-profit sale was made by the customer to the bank, this is where the profit (i.e: the guaranteed amount of the return) was agreed upon. This is a straight-forward Murabaha sale where the customer is selling a commodity to the bank (via the bank's subsidiary) at a price higher than what the customer paid for and the bank agrees to pay the customer (depositor) a profit in installments (deferred payments).

As such, the depositor receives the full agreed upon profit as the guaranteed amount. This is because, in the Tawarruq fixed deposit, there isn't a funds manager relationship established as in Mudarabah which requires profit sharing.

The Purchasing agency relationship established with the bank, or its subsidiary is purely as a means to buy the commodity with an assumption that the bank may be able to negotiate a better deal being able to buy bulk quantities and also to provide a convenience to the depositor.

If it appears that this is a convoluted process, indeed it is. However, it is required to conform to the Shariah principles. In the first example, the Mudaraba fixed deposit conforms to the Shariah principles because there is no interest offered. Both the depositor and the bank share in the profits (mutual risk). Yes, the depositor takes on all the loss if the investment does not make any money, but the bank also has lost its time and money it invested in managing the investment (both parties have their skin in the game). The drawback with Mudaraba fixed deposit is that there is no guarantee of profit. The depositor may lose money if the investments made by the bank do not make profits.

In the case of Tawarruq fixed deposit, the depositor is not taking any risk and is assured of a fixed profit. However, the bank cannot offer this under the Mudaraba contract as it breaks the basic principle of Shariah; that is, the risk and profit should be shared. Therefore, a different approach is applied. By using Murabaha, the bank can offer a predetermined fixed profit to the depositor with the depositor taking no risk.

Note: Such Tawarruq deposits are only permitted by the Shariah Boards if they follow very specific guidelines. For eg: the different relationships (purchasing agent and a sales agent) between the customer and the bank must be clearly and separately executed.

Investments Products

Investment products work very similar to what we have seen already under Mudaraba current account or Mudaraba saving account. In fact, they function the same way in that profits are shared with the fund's manager and losses are borne by the investor with exception; these are investment accounts rather than savings or checking accounts and therefore don't have some of the features that come with savings or checking accounts – e.g.: checkbooks, debit cards etc.

Investment accounts generally are of two types: restricted Mudarabah and unrestricted Mudarabah. Restricted Mudarabah accounts are those where the investor or the depositor (in the case of savings or checking accounts) may restrict how the funds manager invests the funds. That is they may specify that the funds should be invested in certain companies or certain countries etc. Under unrestricted Mudarabah, the fund's manager has the freedom to invest in whatever investments they think is appropriate as long as they comply with the Shariah requirements (e.g.: no investments in liquor or tobacco industries).

Islamic Financing Products

There are many different types of Islamic financing products as there are conventional financing products. What makes it confusing is that in different countries the same Islamic products may be called by different names or spelled differently appearing as though they are completely different products.

The following (Figure 8) are the most common Islamic products in use for corporate finance.

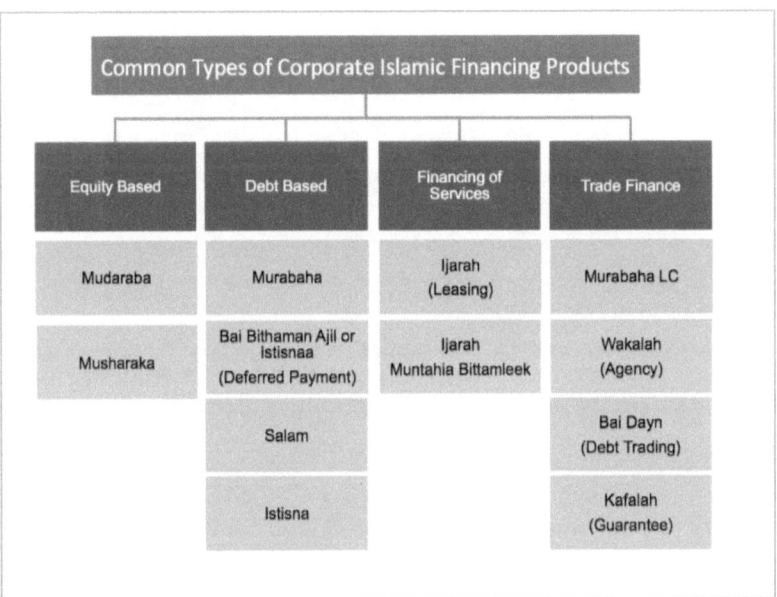

Figure 8

One thing you may have noticed is that the same product names appear under different columns above and even under the deposit accounts that were discussed in the previous chapter. This is because, as mentioned previously, generally the Islamic products are referred to by the same name as underlying Shariah contracts. At the end of this chapter, a contract view, instead of a product view, is shown which indicates which products the contracts support. Perhaps you may find this more useful in your understanding of Islamic products.

49

Equity Based Financing Products

Under Islamic finance, Equity based financing products are also known as contracts of partnerships in that they allow both parties to develop and share in the profits. There are two kinds – Mudaraba and Musharaka.

Mudaraba

Under this product, the bank provides the capital to a Corporate customer and the Corporate customer manages the capital. The corporate and the bank share any profits under a prearranged agreement. However, the bank bears all the risks and if there are any losses, the bank alone absorbs the losses. We have seen how this product operates under the deposit section. The major difference here is that under the deposit section, the investors were the individuals or corporations depositing their funds with a bank, and the bank acted as a fund manager. Under the equity based financing, the roles are reversed. The bank becomes the lender and the individual or the corporation plays the entrepreneur's role. Profit is shared between the company and the bank based on an agreed arrangement. Loss is entirely borne by the bank in that the bank does not make a return on its investment and the loss is absorbed into the business. If the business goes into liquidation, the bank losses all its capital and the company losses its investment in time and effort. If there is any capital gain, the bank is the sole beneficiary of this gain. See Figure 9 below for the flow.

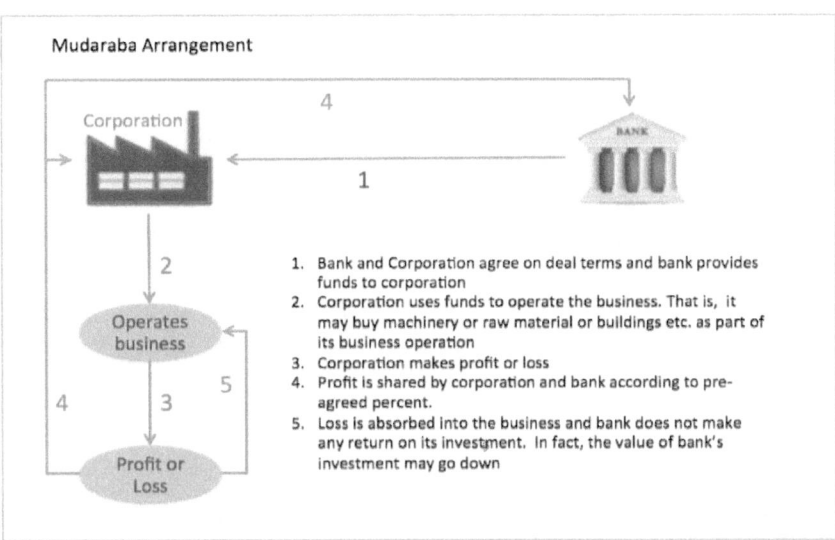

Mudaraba Arrangement

Corporation

BANK

Operates business

Profit or Loss

1. Bank and Corporation agree on deal terms and bank provides funds to corporation
2. Corporation uses funds to operate the business. That is, it may buy machinery or raw material or buildings etc. as part of its business operation
3. Corporation makes profit or loss
4. Profit is shared by corporation and bank according to pre-agreed percent.
5. Loss is absorbed into the business and bank does not make any return on its investment. In fact, the value of bank's investment may go down

Figure 9

Musharaka

In Arabic, Musharaka literally means sharing. From a business context Musharaka means a joint enterprise in which all the partners invest and share the profit or loss of the joint venture.

It is very different from a conventional financing sense in that, in conventional financing the focus is on the interest or rate of return. The lender providing the financing is mostly interested in ensuring the borrower's ability to make the interest and principal payments. The lender may not actively get involved in the operation of the business. The borrower has complete independence and is free to make any business decisions including ones that are detrimental to the business.

On the other hand, Musharaka does not include a fixed profit rate. Rather, the return in Musharaka is based on the actual profit earned by the joint venture. Under conventional financing, generally, the lender in an interest-bearing loan does not suffer loss if the borrower's business is not making money as the borrower is expected to continue to make the installment payment. Of course, if the business goes bust, the lender may lose money but usually the financier has collateral to cover for such situations. Under Musharaka however, if the joint venture fails to make money, the investors also suffer losses since they may not get the installment payment.

Under Shariah, interest is seen as unjust because it results in injustice either to the lender or the borrower. From an Islamic perspective, if the borrower suffers a loss, it is not fair on the part of the lender to claim interest payment; on the other hand, if the borrower makes a huge profit, it is not fair that the borrower continues to pay the lender only a small portion of the profits. Islam is about equal distribution of wealth.

A frequently cited example goes something like this. Let's suppose a depositor deposits $100,000 with a bank under a conventional banking program. The bank agrees to pay a 5% fixed interest rate per annum to the depositor. Let's say the bank takes this money and lends it to other customers and generates a 30% return. The bank is only obligated to pay the depositor 5% and it keeps 25% for itself. The bank in this case had used someone else's money and made huge profits but the depositor whose money was actually used made only a 5% profit.

Thus, in Islam, interest is seen as one of the causes for disproportionate distribution of wealth, which has a tendency to favor the rich against the interests of the poor.

On the other hand, if the bank lost 20% on the investment, it is still obligated to pay the investor 5% interest therefore losing a total of 15%. But overall it is viewed that the interest works against the interests of the poor or desperate.

Under Islamic finance, if a business earns enormous profits, the business cannot keep all of it exclusively; it will have to share it with depositors or investors. Towards this philosophy, the product Musharaka has a tendency to eliminate or reduce the disproportionate distribution of wealth: it tends to favor the common people rather than the rich only.

According to Musharaka principles, a lender must determine whether he is advancing a loan to help the borrower on humanitarian grounds or if the lender desires to share in the profits. If the lender wants to help the borrower on humanitarian grounds, the lender should not claim any profit or any amount in excess of what was lent. However, if the lender wants to get a share in the profits, the lender must also be prepared to share the losses. Thus, the lender and the borrower have a stake in the business and their returns are tied together, the greater the profits from the business, the higher the rate of return to the lender. See Figure 10 below for the flow.

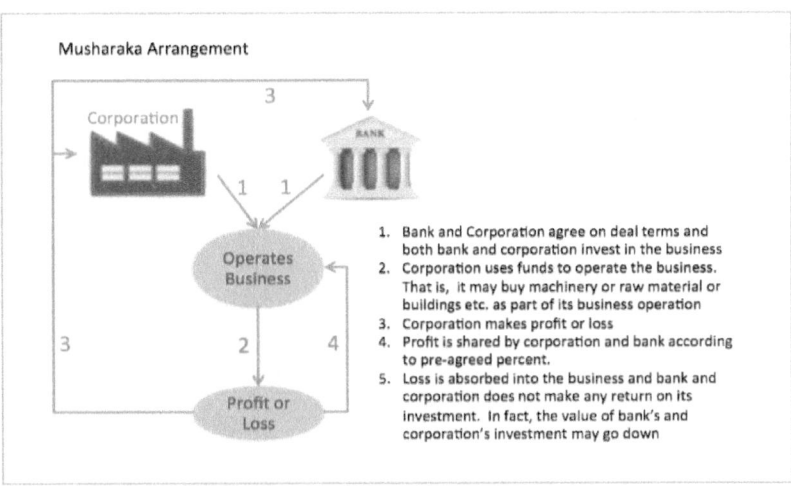

Figure 10

The differences between Musharaka and Mudaraba can be summarized as follows:

• The investment in Musharaka comes from all the partners including the corporation that is seeking investment, while in Mudaraba investment is the sole responsibility of the investor.

• In Musharaka, all the partners may participate in the management of the business and can work for it, while in Mudaraba, the investor (bank) is not allowed to participate in the management of the business.

• In Musharaka, all of the partners share the loss to the extent of the ratio of their investment. In Mudaraba any loss incurred is borne by the investor (bank) only. Also, under Mudaraba, the only loss the corporation incurs is restricted to the expenses it incurred in operating the business. This is assuming that the corporation has applied proper due diligence in carrying out its business activities. If it can be proven that the corporation has not done proper due diligence or has committed dishonesty, the corporation will solely be liable for the loss caused by its negligence or misconduct.

• The partners in Musharaka are on the hook for all the liabilities of the corporation and not just their investment. Therefore, if the business goes into liquidation and it owes more than what it invested, all the exceeding liabilities must be borne by all the partners according to the ratio of their investment unless the partners agree to different terms initially. In the case of Mudaraba, the liability of the investor is usually limited to his investment, unless the investor has given permission to the corporation to incur additional debts on his behalf.

- In Musharaka, the capital and assets become a joint pool. For instance, let's say two partners agree to invest 50/50 shares in a business. If one partner contributed cash of $50,000 and another contributed a building of equal value ($50,000), both these assets are combined into a pool and both the partners own them equally. If the cash is depleted but the building appreciates in value from $50,000 to $75,000, both partners share in the appreciation of the building asset and share in the loss of the cash. In Mudaraba, the bank solely owns all the assets and the corporation only makes money if the business turns a profit. If the business does not make any money but the value of the assets goes up, only the bank tends to gain from this gain.

Diminishing Musharaka

A recent variant of Musharaka financing is called 'Diminishing Musharaka'. Under this product, a bank and a company participate in the joint ownership of a property or equipment or in a joint commercial enterprise. Both the investor and the company invest in the business according to an agreed percent. The difference lies in this: the investor's contribution is divided into a number of distinct units which the company will purchase from time to time thus increasing its share of investment in the business while the share of the investment from the investor goes down equally eventually making the company the sole owner of the investment.

The Diminishing Musharaka concept is implemented in different forms. One example is shown below:

Let's assume a business wants to purchase machinery to operate its business worth $100,000. The company approaches a bank for financing and the bank and the company agrees to a 60/40 split. Bank invests $60,000 and the company $40,000. Thus, the bank owns 60% of the machinery asset and the company owns 40%. The company agrees to pay the bank an agreed upon "rent" for the use of the asset. At the same time, the share of the bank may be divided into 6 equal slices of $10,000 each. As part of this agreement, the company agrees to buy out each equal part of the bank's investment every month. So, at the end of the first month, the company pays the bank $10,000 for the first slice. Thus, at the end of the first month, the company's share in the asset goes up from 40% to 50% and the bank's share in the asset decreases from 60% to 50%. This cycle repeats where at the end of 6 months, the company buys out the bank's share and owns the asset outright. As the company purchases each slice, the rent it pays to the bank proportionally goes down each month until at the end of 6 months the company does not owe the bank any rent as it fully owns the asset.

Debt Based Financing Products

Debt based financing products are also known as contracts of exchange or trade. There are four kinds that are commonly used – Murabaha, Al Bai Bithaman Ajil (BBA), Salam and Istisna.

Murabaha Finance

This is the most common Islamic financing product used by banks today. Thus, this term has become ubiquitous in business circles today as a method of bank financing whereas the traditional legal construct of Murabaha was very different.

Murabaha in its traditional definition, in fact, refers to a kind of sale that has nothing to do with financing. If a buyer agrees to purchase a specific commodity at a price that was based on cost plus profit, it is called a Murabaha transaction. The basic requirement of a Murabaha transaction is that the seller must disclose the actual cost they have incurred in acquiring the commodity, and then he may add some profit on top of it. The profit amount may be a lump sum amount (e.g.: $1,000) or it may be determined as a percentage of the original cost (e.g.: 10% of cost). The payment in the case of traditional Murabaha must be made immediately. There is no financing involved.

Disclosing the actual cost incurred by the seller and how much profit the seller is going to charge is one of the main features distinguishing it from other kinds of sale. If a seller sells a commodity without any reference to the cost, it is not considered a Murabaha sale, even if the seller discloses the profit to the buyer. Therefore, Murabaha, in its original form, is a simple sale.

In cases where a deferred payment is set up, a product called Al Bai Bithaman Ajil (BBA) or "Bai Muajjal" (discussed below) is used in combination with Murabaha sale. This product is generally known as Murabaha Finance.

Remember: Murabaha Sale Plus BBA (or Bai muajjal) is Murabaha Finance

Many Islamic scholars do not agree that such transactions are valid under Shariah even if they meet the requirements of Murabaha. However, many other scholars agree that they do indeed meet the requirements of Shariah. While this controversy and disagreement continues, Murabaha transactions dominate in the Islamic banking space and comprise over 80% of all Islamic finance transactions.

Al Bai Bithaman Ajil (BBA) or Bai Muajjal

Al Bai Bithaman Ajil means a "deferred payment sale" or a credit sale. This is also known as "Bai Muajjal" or "Bai Nassiah". It is a mode of Islamic financing used for financing consumer goods as well as corporate trade. As mentioned under Murabaha Finance above, deferred payment sale (credit sale) is combined with Murabaha sale in order to facilitate financing under Murabaha. Note this is similar to what we have seen already under Tawarraq Fixed Deposits; the only difference is that the buyer in this case is the individual or company wanting financing.

This is similar in concept under conventional finance where a buyer may purchase goods from a seller using a sales contract and turn to the bank for financing under a financing contract. These two contracts could be combined and executed together or separately. In fact, under conventional finance these two contracts may be executed in any sequence. That is, the buyer may apply for financing first and then buy the goods or buy the goods and then apply for financing.

Under Murabaha finance these contracts are executed together but in a specific sequence. Under Al Bai Bithaman Ajil (BBA) the following requirements must be met:

- The due date of the payment should be fixed in a clear and concise manner. For e.g.: the due date payment can be fixed at a particular date (say Nov 10, 2017), or by specifying a period, like three months, but it cannot be fixed with reference to a future event for which the exact date is unknown or is uncertain. For e.g.: the future date of payment cannot be specified as when the buyer is able to sell the goods and collect funds. Since, this cannot be precisely determined, this sale becomes void.

- If the deferred price is more than the cash price, it must be fixed at the time of sale. Once the price is fixed, it cannot be decreased in case of earlier payment, nor can it be increased in case of default. As such, variable rate financing where the installment amount could vary each month cannot be offered under Shariah.

- Since penalty for late payment is not allowed under Shariah, the buyers may be asked to donate a specified amount for a charitable purpose. In cases where the seller does receive such donations, he is obligated to pass this on to charitable causes and not to count this as income.

- If the commodity is sold on installments, the seller may put a condition on the buyer that if he fails to pay any installment on its due date, the remaining installments will become due immediately. The seller may also ask for collateral to mitigate the risk of the buyer defaulting on his payments.

So, Al Bai Bithaman Ajil or BBA sets some specific rules or conditions for deferred payments which can be paid in full at a future date or paid in installments at pre-agreed amounts and dates.

What makes Murabaha Financing Legitimate under Shariah Law?

The basic rules for sale we encountered earlier are required to make any sale valid. If any of the above rules are not met, the sale becomes invalid. Keep in mind, Murabaha is purely a sales contract and has nothing to do with financing. By extending Murabaha with a deferred payment option (BBA and Bai Muajjal), banks have devised a way to finance commodity purchases. Now let us see what are the conditions that must be met to make the financing part valid under Murabaha.

But, before we look at the conditions, let's first look at some of the basic steps in Murabaha financing:

1. Let's assume a Buyer wants to purchase a car.

2. The Buyer decides what make and model he wants to buy and from which dealer he wants to buy.

3. Let's say the cost of this car is $10,000.

4. The Buyer wants to finance this purchase and goes to his Bank for financing.

5. The Buyer provides his bank all the details about the car that he wishes to purchase.

6. The Bank conducts due diligence on the Buyer to assess his credit risk.

7. The Buyer and Bank agree on a profit margin and agree on the number and amount of installments. Let's say the profit margin is $2000 and the number of installments is 12. The total amount due to the bank is $12,000 payable over 12 months at $1,000 per month.

8. The Bank buys the car from the car dealer for $10,000.

9. The Bank turns around and sells the car to the Buyer at the agreed upon price of $12,000 to be paid in installments of $1,000 each month for 12 months.

10. The Buyer owns the car and immediately makes use of it and makes the installment payments to the Bank for the next 12 months.

11. The Buyer got what he wanted immediately; the Bank made a profit of $2,000.

At first sight this may seem like a convoluted process to someone who is familiar with conventional financing. In the conventional example, once the bank agrees to finance the purchase (presumably after conducting due diligence on the buyer), the bank gives the money to the buyer or to the car dealer directly. The bank does not purchase the car and therefore never "owns" it. The buyer gets the money from the bank and goes and makes the purchase.

In fact, the above scenarios may be even simpler where the buyer selects a car he/she wants and applies for a loan right at the car dealer and the bank may approve the credit after conducting due diligence.

Conditions that must be met
From an Islamic finance point of view, the Murabaha finance must adhere to several key components that are required. These are:

a) Because Murabaha is a sales contract, all the sales rules mentioned earlier under Murabaha sale must also be met in the Murabaha financing deal. And in our above scenario they do. For example:

b) The funds from the financing must be used to purchase the commodity agreed in the deal. The funds from a Murabaha financing cannot be diverted for other purposes. In our scenario this condition is met as the bank first buys the car and then sells it to the buyer. Alternatively, the bank may appoint an agent to buy the car but even in this case the bank is the actual "owner" of the car. Note: the agent appointed by the bank could be the buyer himself. However, the buyer is transacting in the name of the bank and not himself. In this case the buyer does not own the car at this point. The Banks may do this in cases where they have to rely on the expertise of the buyer to verify the specifications of the car.

c) The lender must have owned the item being sold. In our scenario the bank purchased the car and therefore "owned" it before selling it to the buyer.

d) In addition, the commodity must be bought from a third party and not the Buyer himself. In other words, a customer cannot approach the bank and ask the bank to buy a commodity from him and turn around and buy it back from the bank at a higher price and make payments in installments to the bank thereby financing the commodity. This is called a "buy-back" deal and is not allowed under Murabaha.

e) The lender must have taken possession of the item either physically or in title. More importantly, the risk must transfer to the lender. The risk may be loss incurred due to natural causes (e.g.: fire) or loss of value due to market conditions or external factors. In some cases, the bank may appoint the buyer as his agent wherein the buyer purchases the items on behalf of the bank even though the buyer will eventually buy them back from the bank. The bank may do this because the buyer has specific knowledge or expertise in determining the condition of the item being bought. The important thing to remember is that while the item is in buyer's possession, the risk must still remain with the bank. If something happens to the item in buyer's possession, the bank is liable for the damages or loss. That is, the bank is still the owner and the buyer is acting simply as the lender's agent. When the bank sells the item to the buyer, the risk shifts to the buyer.

f) The deferred payment amount and the installment amount and dates have been pre-agreed.

As can be seen from above, Murabaha finance meets some of the basic principles of Shariah. Because the bank is taking possession of the item, the bank may ensure that the item is of good quality or worth the cost. Also, the fact that the bank is purchasing the item first also eliminates some speculation from the market. For instance, the buyer cannot agree to pay over and above the market value of the item simply because he desperately wants it and has bid up the price. Since the bank is purchasing the item first, the bank may perform market research to ensure the cost being paid is reasonable, especially since the bank may get stuck with it if the buyer walks away.

Another thing to watch under Murabaha is that there are actually different stages the financing deals goes through and different contracts may apply wherein the roles that each party plays may change. Therefore, it is important to keep these different contracts and roles distinct and separate and not mix them up. Otherwise, the Murabaha contract may be seen as void. For e.g.: During the initial stages where the Buyer and the bank reach an agreement where the bank agrees to buy the commodity and sell it to the buyer, there is only a promise made to buy and sell a commodity. There is no actual sale since no commodity changed hands. Thus, at this stage there are only a promisor and promisee: not a seller and a buyer. This changes into a buyer and seller relationship when the bank sells the commodity to the buyer.

These roles may change again when the installment payment agreement goes into effect that sets up a creditor and debtor relationship. At this point the bank may ask the buyer to furnish a security deposit or a collateral. This collateral must only take effect during the financing stage and not before. One has to be careful in executing these contracts and keep them separate and distinct even though these may be executed together.

Some Basic Mistakes in Deferred Payment Finance

As mentioned before, the deferred payment finance products have to conform to strict requirements to be legitimate under Shariah. Therefore, banks must watch out for the common errors in the practical implementation of the deferred payment finance (aka Murabaha Finance). These include:

a) The most common error is that Murabaha finance is used for financing non-commodity related expenses such as payment of salaries, rent and other expenses. Commodity Murabaha is the best product for such financing.

b) Banks must exercise caution that funds are used for purchase of specific commodities. Sometimes borrowers may specify a fictitious commodity that they never intend to purchase and would prefer to use the funds for something else. Banks must ensure the funds are used for purpose specified in the contract either by purchasing the commodity themselves or by paying directly to the supplier or by inspecting the goods purchased.

c) The banks must ensure that the various different contracts involved in the financing are signed and executed in proper sequence. For instance, if the borrower is signing the entire document set in one go, there is a risk that the ownership of the goods never transferred to the bank legitimately and therefore the entire sale may not conform to Murabaha requirement.

d) Banks must ensure that the buyer has not already purchased the commodity before applying for financing under Murabaha finance. As mentioned before, buy-back sale is prohibited under Murabaha.

You maybe wondering how paying a lower price for cash sale and a higher price for deferred payment isn't the same as charging interest. Because this increase in price is purely due to the fact that the payment is paid later, one may argue that this increase is purely against time that makes it analogous to interest payment.

This argument maybe based on the misunderstanding or assumption that whenever there is a price change taking the time of payment into consideration, this difference in price is interest. This presumption is not valid. This is because under Sharia, _excess amount charged against future payment is considered interest only where money is being lent_. If a commodity is sold in exchange of money, the seller may take into consideration different factors when fixing the price including the time of payment. Therefore a seller may charge a higher price and the purchaser may agree to pay higher price due to various reasons.

However, the seller may in the beginning consider time factor in determining the price, but once both the seller and the buyer agree to the price, the time element is no longer involved. Thus, if the the buyer fails to make the payment on the stipulated date, the seller cannot charge a different price. The seller cannot say, pay me next month but at a higher price. The price remains fixed. Under conventional terms, if the buyer does not pay on time, the seller may charge him penalty and additional interest for the delay in payment. This is not allowed under Islamic finance. Once the price is fixed upfront, it cannot be increased even if the buyer fails to make payment on time. Also, penalty cannot be changed if the buyer fails to make a payment. Because of these stipulations, the increase in price due to delayed payment is not considered an interest.

Bay Salam

Bay Salam is a contract for where advanced payment is made for goods to be delivered later. Bay Salam is generally used to finance agricultural goods. Generally accepted conditions for bay Salam are that:

1. The goods sold need not be in existence at the time of sale.

2. The delivery date and location must be specified.

3. Full advance settlement of the agreed trade price is required at the time of sale contracting.

4. The quality of the items to be delivered should be defined. Items must be fungible in nature. Hence, rare items, or those that are not precisely specifiable cannot be included in the bay Salam contract. If the quality of the items upon delivery is not what was specified, the buyer has the right of refusal.

5. The quantity of the items to be delivered should be defined and fixed according to the normal method of measurement of those items and should not depend upon unforeseeable factors. The quantity of goods purchased under the bay Salam contract cannot for example be defined as that resulting from the cultivation of a given plot of land since such a quantity may vary according to unforeseeable factors.

6. The buyer does not enjoy ownership of the goods until delivery has taken place.

7. The buyer has the right to take surety from the seller as a form of performance bond.

8. Where the seller is unable to produce the contracted items on the delivery date, the buyer may nullify the bay Salam contract and exercise the performance bond.

9. The seller may deliver the contracted items irrespective of the buyer's circumstances on the delivery date.

Istisna (manufacturing contracts)

Istisna is a contract agreement for financing of manufactured goods and commodities (as opposed to Bay Salam where financing is for agricultural goods) where the payment is made in advance for goods to be delivered later. Istisna is typically used in the financing the manufacturing or construction of homes, factories, bridges, roads, highways, airports and other major construction projects. Under Istisna, the exact specification of the goods to be manufactured must be specified and the exact price must be paid at the time of contract or at a later date. The contract may be canceled before the manufacture of goods starts only if both parties agree. Once the manufacture of goods is in process, the contract cannot be canceled.

Islamic Banking and International Trade (Imports and Exports)

Due to globalization, international trade has become a key component for most businesses including small and medium enterprises. Companies find it sometimes cheaper to source from foreign locations than from local suppliers. And in some cases, the goods a company is sourcing may not be even available locally. Therefore, the company has no choice but to source from overseas suppliers. Globalization has opened up sources and suppliers all over the world for companies to import from.

Likewise, globalization has opened the world markets to companies that are selling their wares. Instead of selling in the local markets or in the domestic markets, companies can export their goods to buyers located all over the globe. The following graphic from the World Trade Organization represents how important international trade has become. As you can see (Figure 11), in 2013, the total global exports were a whooping $18trillion!

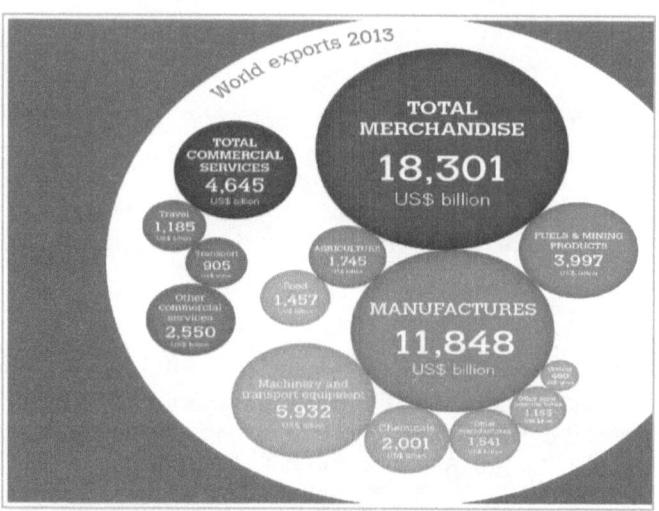

Figure 11

Truly, globalization has brought the world a lot closer for trading.

Having said this, the problem is that the buyers and suppliers are still physically separated from each other. This lack of geographical proximity between buyers and sellers means there is a time lag between when the goods are shipped and when the goods are received/delivered. For example: if one were to source goods from the local market, one would visit the seller's shop, select the goods one wants, pay for them and bring them home or have them delivered within a day or two. This is not the case if sourcing from suppliers located in different countries. It may take anywhere from a few days to several weeks from the time the goods are shipped to when they arrive at the buyer's location.

Thus, one of the basic rules of a valid sale under islamic banking - the sale must be absolute and immediate (Rule #4) - cannot be met. Consequently, for all practical purposes, the basic transaction in international trade is technically not a regular Murabaha sale but a forward sales transaction. That is, either Bai Muajjal or Bai Salam or Istisna. However, keep in mind, under Islamic finance generally the normal Murabaha sales contracts are combined with Bai Maujjai or Bai Salam contracts and collectively known as Murabaha Finance.

In addition, four other key factors complicate matters in international trade. First, because the buyers and sellers are generally located in different countries it introduces an element of risk since the buyers and sellers may not know each other or may not have even met face to face. Even though eventually the buyers and sellers may build up a trusting relationship, in the early stages, the seller may want advance payment before he ships the goods as he wants to avoid the risk of shipping the goods and not getting paid. The buyer, on the other hand, may not want to make advance payment since there is a risk that the seller may not ship the goods on time, or may not ship at all.

Secondly, there is a risk that the goods shipped may not be what the buyer ordered. The seller may ship the wrong goods, the wrong quantity or ship goods that do not meet buyer's specifications. This places the buyer at a disadvantage since he is not able to inspect the goods before they are shipped. In addition, there is a risk that the goods may get damaged during shipment. If they do get damaged, who is liable for them? If there is insurance involved, then who pays for the insurance? Who actually owns the goods while they are in transit? These questions, if not clearly addressed, could lead to serious consequences for the buyers and sellers.

Thirdly, there may be different legal systems involved in different countries which the buyers and sellers may not be familiar with. In addition, there may be different customs requirements, different regulatory and different compliance requirements in different countries which the buyers and sellers may not be familiar with.

And finally, there may be different currencies involved requiring foreign exchange conversion, which adds an element of foreign exchange risk. For e.g.: Let's say the buyer's currency is "AED" and the seller's currency is "HKD". The buyer agrees to pay HKD 100,000 sixty days after receiving the goods. On the day the goods were received, the exchange rate between AED to HKD was 2.11. That is, one AED would fetch 2.11 HKD. So, the actual cost in AED to the buyer is actually AED 47,393.36. Let's assume that in 60 days when the payment is due, the currency rate drifted significantly, and the new exchange rate is 1.80 instead of 2.11. Because of this, the cost for the buyer goes up. Instead of costing AED 47,393.36, the same goods now cost the buyer AED 55,555.55. A difference of AED 8,162.19! That is a significant cost increase indeed. And this increase in cost resulted not because the seller changed his price but simply because the exchange rate changed. If the exchange rate went the other way, instead of 1.80, let's say it went to 2.30, the seller would be disadvantaged in this case. In order to avoid this risk, the vast majority of global trade is denominated in stable currencies such as USD. Over 80% of the global trade is denominated in USD as it is considered a very stable currency, which does not fluctuate much as compared to other currencies. But the risk does not go away as eventually both the buyers and sellers have to convert from USD to their local currencies.

These factors give rise to uncertainty to both buyer and seller and increase the element of risk for both. Therefore, due to this uncertainty (Gharar) the conventional international products involved in facilitating trade cannot be used under Islamic banking. They have to be modified to fit under the Shariah requirements. But, before we look at the Islamic trade products, let's first review the conventional trade products so they provide a context when we discuss the Islamic counterparts.

The Role of Banks in Trade

Banks play a key role in facilitating trade. Using various products depending on buyers and sellers' requirements, the banks play the role of middlemen between buyers and sellers. The banks can provide assurance to the seller that if the seller meets the conditions set out by the buyer and the bank, the bank will pay the seller irrespective of what the buyer says.

Likewise, the bank can provide assurance to the buyer that the goods shipped by the seller meet the requirements of the buyer since the banks can check the documents provided by the seller and the shipping companies. By checking, or examining, these documents the bank can assure the buyer that the goods meet the requirements of the buyer.

There are many products banks offer to buyers and sellers to facilitate international trade including Letter of Credits (L/C), Documentary Collections and Open Account.

The Logistics of International Trade

International trade begins with a sales contract between exporters (sellers) and importers (buyers). This contract governs the obligations and responsibilities of buyers and sellers. Among other things, a sales contract may specify detailed description of goods, the quantity and price of merchandise, the currency of payment and the payment terms, from where the goods are to be shipped and to which port they are to be delivered and by what timeframe the goods are to be delivered.

The ownership of goods is controlled through a "Bill of Lading" (also known as B/L) issued by the shipping company to the seller. A Bill of Lading conveys title to the goods. The buyer needs the Bill of Lading to pick up the goods when they arrive. Since the shipping company issues the B/L to the seller, the B/L must "travel" to the buyer so the buyer can collect the goods. Depending on how the sale is structured and what bank products are being used in this trade, the B/L may take a complicated path before it eventually reaches the buyer (more on this later).

If the Bill of Lading is non-negotiable, it is generally assigned to the buyer. In the case of a negotiable bill of lading, the title (or ownership) to the goods can be transferred to another party through endorsement. This is an important point we will discuss later since "owning" the goods is a significant consideration in Islamic finance.

The actual payment is facilitated by the way of a "Draft" or a Bill of Exchange or via cash payment in advance or payment in cash upon submission of an invoice (as in "Open Account").

A Draft is an unconditional written demand by the exporter (seller) for payment. A Draft is drawn either on the buyer or on the buyer's bank that assumes the legal obligation to pay. The Draft also indicates when the payment is due. This is known as the tenor or maturity date of a draft. A Draft marked "at sight" is to be paid immediately upon presentation of the draft.

The seller or the seller's bank that created the Draft is known as the Drawee and the buyer on whom the Draft is drawn on is known as the Drawer.

A Draft with a payment due date in the future (after presentation) is known as a "time draft" or a "Usance" draft. The payment due date, or tenor, usually depends on the time necessary for goods to reach their destination, to be sold by the buyer and the proceeds becoming available to buyers to pay for the goods. The tenor of a time draft may be stated as "60 days sight". This means the payment is due 60 days after presentation of the draft to the buyer or the bank by the seller. The "presentation" date of the draft to the buyer or the bank may be several days after the seller created the draft. For instance, let's say a seller in Hong Kong prepares the draft today and couriers it to a buyer in Dubai. The draft may not reach the buyer in Dubai until a week from today. Therefore, the "presentation" date will be a week from today and consequently the payment date will be 60 days from presentation date (not from when the draft was created).

Release of Bill of Lading (title to goods) to the buyer only happens after the Draft is presented and paid or "accepted". If the draft is payable "at sight", the buyer is expected to pay the seller at which point the B/L is released to the buyer who can collect the goods.

If the Draft is a "Usance" bill or a time draft, the draft must be "Accepted" by the buyer or buyer's bank. The buyer or the bank writes "Accepted" on the Draft and signs and dates the Draft. This process is known as accepting the draft and is an acknowledgement by the buyer or buyer's bank of their obligation to pay on the due date. This is similar to an IOU or a promise to pay. After acceptance, the B\L is released to the buyer. The payment due date clock starts ticking from the date of acceptance.

Drafts become negotiable instruments if they are made payable to order or to bearer. That is, they can be sold by endorsing the Draft to another party. This party may then sell the Draft to someone else by endorsing it again. There is no limit to the number of times a Draft can be sold and resold. The party that holds the Draft (called holder in due course) when it becomes due collects the payment from the buyer or buyer's bank by presenting the Draft for payment.

The buyer (the Drawer) has an unconditional obligation to pay the Draft upon presentation on or after the maturity date. If the buyer or buyer's bank does not pay the Draft, the current holder of the Draft has recourse through all previous endorsers back to the original seller of the Draft (the seller or the seller's bank).

Payment Options under International Trade

Note: if you are already familiar with the payment options discussed below, you may skip to the chapter called "Financing International Trade".

As mentioned earlier, the payment options under international trade depend on the relationship the buyer and seller have established or depends on their financing needs that may require the use of specific trade finance products as a way to enable financing. The most common payment are:

1. Open Account
2. Documentary Collection
3. Letter of Credit (L/C)
4. Cash in Advance

The following risk ladder (Figure 12) shows the payment options and the risks associated with them for the exporter (seller) and the importer (buyer).

Figure 12

Open Account

Open Account payment method is where the seller ships the goods, and the buyer generally pays 60 or 90 days (or longer) after picking up the goods. This provides enough time for the buyer to sell the goods and collect the funds in order to pay the seller. The payment risk is the highest to the seller since the seller is shipping the goods without assurance of getting paid. On the other hand, the payment risk is the lowest to the buyer since the buyer does not have to pay until he receives the goods and has enough time to sell them and collect funds. Over 85% of international trade is conducted using Open Accounts. This option is generally used where the buyer and seller have established a trusting relationship or where the buyer is a very reputable company, and the sellers generally trust them.

Cash in Advance

Cash advance is made at a very early stage in the process. This is because the seller wants assurance that the buyer is serious and has the capacity to make payment before he starts making the goods. Cash in advance gives advantage to the seller by eliminating the payment risk but adds the shipment risk to the buyer in that the seller may not ship the goods after he receives the cash in advance. Also, the buyer may face cash flow issues as the payment is made well in advance from when the goods are received and sold.

The Letter of Credit

A Letter of Credit (also known as an L/C) is a written obligation issued by a bank for the benefit of the seller (exporter) at the request of a buyer (importer). In L/C terminology, the buyer is called an "Applicant" because the buyer is submitting an application to their bank to "issue" the L/C. The seller is called a "Beneficiary" because he gets the benefit of the L/C. That is, ultimately the seller gets paid if they meet all the conditions specified in the L/C.

The following (Figure 13) represents a simplified process of issuing an L/C

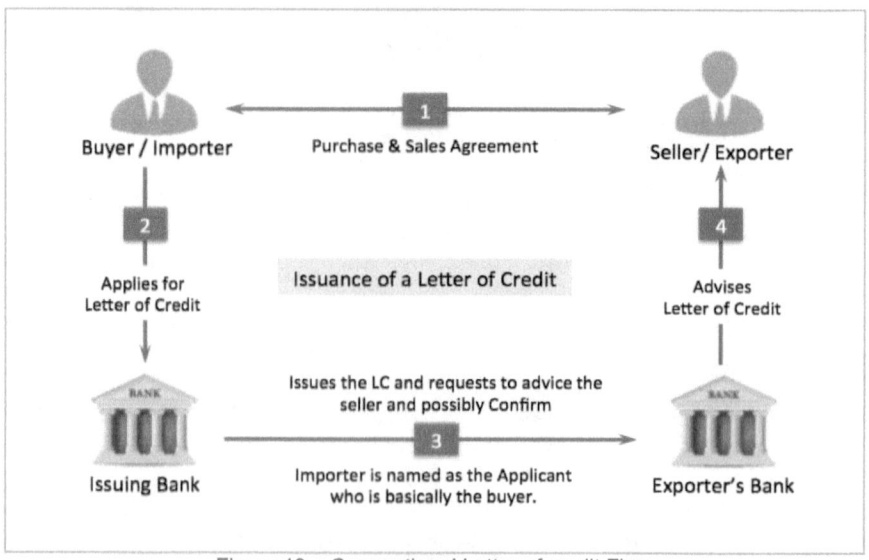

Figure 13 – Conventional Letter of credit Flow

The application that the buyer submits to the bank includes details of the sales contract between the buyer and the seller as well as all the terms and conditions that both buyer and seller agreed to including, the expiry date, by when to ship the goods, which port to ship them to, who pays for the freight and insurance etc.

The buyer bank reviews the application to ensure it meets its requirements and standards and the bank "issues" the L/C. Thus, the bank that issues the L/C is called an "Issuing bank". By issuing the L/C, the bank assumes the legal obligation to pay the beneficiary (seller), if the seller meets all the conditions as mentioned in the L/C, including presentation of the required documents as prescribed in the L/C. This "issued" L/C is delivered to the seller directly by the buyer's bank or via an intermediary called Advising Bank. At this point, for all practical purposes, the L/C becomes a contract between the buyer's bank and the seller. From this point forward, the seller deals with the bank in submitting documents and to get paid. The buyer's bank is obligated to make the payment to the seller if the seller meets his obligations as mentioned in the L/C regardless if the buyer agrees or not.

The following (Figure 14) represents a simplified process of payment under an L/C:

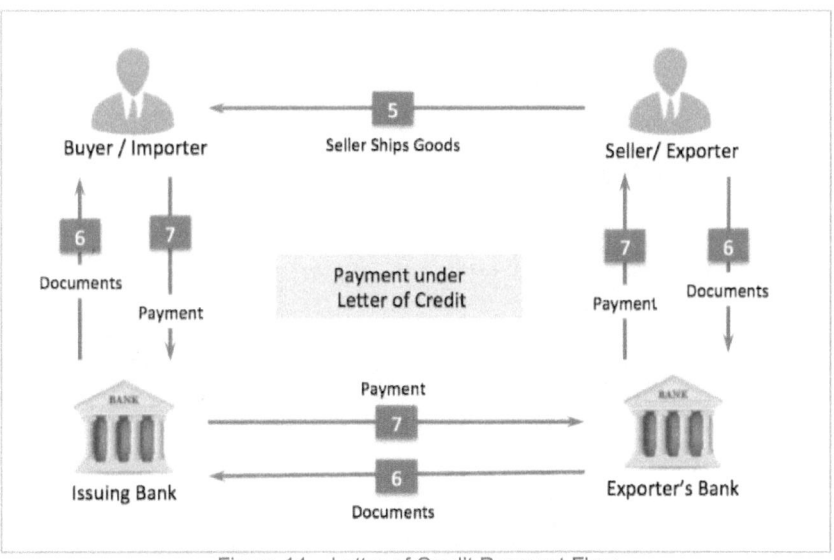

Figure 14 – Letter of Credit Payment Flow

The Draft is included as part of the documents submitted by the seller to the bank. The tenor of the Draft must correspond to credit terms mentioned in the L/C. The Draft can be a sight Draft or a Usance bill.

Now, you may be wondering why the bank would take this obligation to pay the seller regardless of what happens to the buyer (assuming the seller meets the requirements mentioned in the L/C)? In other words, why would the bank take this risk? The bank may or may not. If the buyer is a new startup and has not established a credit, the bank may require the buyer to deposit cash (or some other asset) as collateral before the bank issues the L/C. This way if the buyer does not pay when the payment under the L/C becomes due, the bank has access to the collateral. In this case, the bank is taking no risk at all.

But generally, the buyer has an established line of credit with the bank and uses this line of credit to issue the L/C. The bank reduces the line of credit available to the buyer by the amount of the L/C and issues the L/C. For example, if the L/C amount is $1million and the buyer has an available line of credit of $10million, the bank reduces the available line of credit to $9million and issues the $1million L/C.

This exposes the bank to commercial credit risk of the buyer. To mitigate this risk, the bank may have the B/L consigned in its name. By doing this, the bank will be the owner of the goods up to the time when the documents are transferred to the importer. Thus, if the buyer does not pay the bank, the bank at least has the goods in its name and can sell them to recoup some of the funds.

Once the bank receives the documents from the seller, the bank "examines" the documents to ensure they conform to the conditions specified in the L/C. Some of these conditions include checking the inspection certificates and the packing lists to ensure the right goods with proper specification were shipped. If the bank finds everything satisfactorily, the bank notifies the buyer that documents have arrived in clean condition and that the payment is due if the terms are on sight. The seller would have submitted a Draft payable at sight. At this point the bank is obligated to make the payment even if the buyer is unable to do so.

If the terms of payment are 60 days by deferred, a Draft is not submitted, and the seller has to wait 60 days from the time the bank examines the documents and finds them clean. The seller submits a Draft at the end of 60 days for payment which essentially becomes a sight payment at that point.

In case the terms of payment are 60 days by "acceptance", the seller submits a Usance Draft that stipulates payment to be made in 60 days once the issuing bank (or its nominated bank) "accepts" the Draft. This accepted Draft may be sold or discounted by the seller if the seller wishes to get funds earlier.

So far what we have described is a simple L/C process using only four parties – the importer, the exporter, the issuing bank and the advising bank. In practice however, the L/C process may get complex and may involve several other parties such as, the negotiating bank, the reimbursing bank, freight forwarder, document preparers etc.

The following diagram (Figure 15) shows some of the common parties involved in a L/C transaction and the typical process flow under a Letter of Credit. Description of each step follows

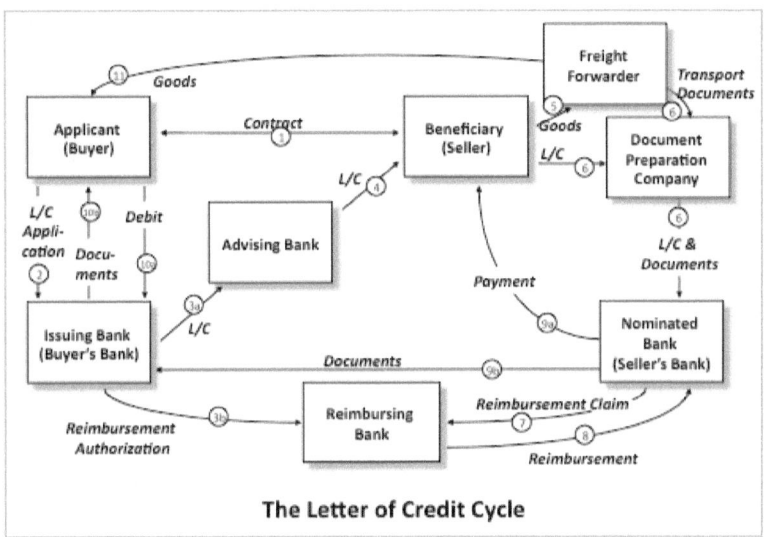

The Letter of Credit Cycle

Figure 15 – Letter of Credit Life Cycle

Step 1 - The buyer agrees to purchase goods from the seller using a letter of credit as the mechanism of payment.

Step 2 - The buyer applies to his bank (buyers bank or the issuing bank) for a letter of credit using a letter of credit application form.

Step 3a - After approving the application, the issuing bank issues the actual letter of credit instrument and forwards it to an advising bank (generally the seller's bank) to be "advised" to the seller.

Step 3b – Optionally, at the time the L/C is sent to the advising bank, the issuing bank may also send a reimbursement authorization to their chosen reimbursing bank. This bank is the clearing bank the issuing bank uses when making payments in the currency of the L/C and will play a role when the time comes to pay the L/C.

Step 4 - The advising bank authenticates the letter of credit and delivers it to the seller (beneficiary). Optionally, if the issuing bank has requested them to do so, the advising bank may add their "confirmation" to the L/C (and thereby become the confirming bank).

Step 5 - Having received the issuing bank's assurance of payment (or that of the confirming bank if the L/C has been confirmed), the seller manufactures the goods and delivers goods generally to the freight forwarder, who ships the goods to the buyer.

Step 6 - The seller, the freight forwarder, and/or a document preparation company prepare the documents called for in the letter of credit and present them to the "nominated bank." The letter of credit may nominate a specific bank where documents are to be presented or it may say it is "available with any bank," giving the seller the freedom to choose where to present documents. If the L/C has been confirmed, documents must be presented to the advising/confirming bank.

Step 7 - The nominated bank examines the documents and, if they comply, obtains funds for payment to the beneficiary in accordance with the terms of the letter of credit, generally by sending a reimbursement claim to the reimbursing bank named in the credit.

Step 8 - The reimbursing bank matches the nominated bank's claim against the reimbursement authorizations they are holding, charges the issuing bank's account, and transfers funds to the nominated bank.

Step 9a & b - The nominated bank transfers payment to the seller (beneficiary) and forwards the documents to the issuing bank.

Step 10a & b - The issuing bank examines the documents. If it agrees with the nominated bank that the documents comply with the letter of credit, the issuing bank obtains payment from the buyer (applicant) in accordance with the terms of the applicant's letter of credit agreement and forwards the documents to the buyer.

Step 11 - The applicant (buyer) uses the documents to pick up the merchandise from the carrier, completing the letter of credit cycle.

Notice that in the steps described above, financing was nowhere mentioned. That is because this international trade transaction did not require any financing since in step 10, the issuing bank obtains funds from the buyer. Presumably, the buyer has the funds to pay for the goods.

Documentary Collection

A documentary collection is another commonly used product in international trade that works as follows:

A. The exporter (seller) ships the goods and submits the Draft along with the B/L to his bank.

B. The exporter's bank may either directly or through an intermediary bank approach the importer (buyer) for payment.

C. If the Draft is a "documents against payment" (D/P) draft, the exporter's bank expects payment immediately from the importer or the intermediary bank. When the payment is received, the exporter's bank releases the documents (B/L) to the exporter so they can pick up the goods.

D. If the Draft is a "documents against acceptance" (D/A) draft, the importer "accepts" the Draft by writing "accepted" on the Draft. The importer also dates and signs the Draft thereby creating a trade acceptance and mails the Draft back to the exporter. The exporter in this case is assured that the payment will be made on the maturity date of the Draft. The accepted Draft becomes a negotiable bill of exchange, which can be sold and resold as discussed earlier.

It is important to note that in Documentary Collections, the buyer's bank does not take any obligation as in an L/C. It is simply acting as a middleman handling over the shipping documents to the buyer when the buyer makes the payment. Thus, the exporter is still taking a risk that the importer may not pay since the exporter has shipped the goods. Even though the importer cannot pick up the goods without the shipping documents (which the bank will not release unless the exporter pays), the exporter is still under a loss as the exporter has already shipped the goods, which may be sitting in some warehouse in a foreign port for which the exporter has to pay storage (demurrage) fees.

Note that none of the above mentioned products required any financing. If the buyer pays the amount when due, no matter which product the buyer uses, either L/C or Documentary Collection or Open Account etc, there is simply no need to finance. But no matter which product they end up using, generally, buyers and sellers seek financing to facilitate international trade. And this financing is typically short term in nature (30 to 180 days). For the buyers this is just enough time to receive the goods, sell them and pay off the loan. On the seller's side, the short-term financing may be enough time for the sellers to purchase raw materials to make the goods and ship them and get paid.

Which of the above products the importers and exporter use depend on their relationship and their financing needs. In some cases, even if both the parties have a trusting relationship, they may still decide to use an L/C instead of Open Account, because the exporter may want to avail of easier financing that is possible with an L/C as opposed to Open Account since a bank is guaranteeing the payment under the L/C.

We will look at financing next.

Financing International Trade

The key players in international trade are importer, exporter, the importer's bank and the exporter's bank. During discussion under the products above, we have seen their roles and the risks each of these players undertake. These are summarized as follows:

An importer is in business generally to serve the needs of the community and to make a profit. The importer may not have a shortage of funds or he may be short of funds but hopes to pay the seller after he receives the goods and sells them. The importer also faces risks of non-shipment of goods, damage during transit and foreign exchange rate fluctuations.

The exporter has a good proposition as he is holding a confirmed order from an importer. He may have all necessary funds to start manufacturing the goods. Or the exporter may be short of funds and may be looking for financing to help him manufacture the goods. In addition, even if the exporter has the funds to manufacture the goods, he may not be able to sustain without getting paid for 30, 60 or 90 days after shipping the goods. Since the exporter is holding an accepted Draft from the buyer, he may decide to "discount" this Draft and get paid sooner.

The importer's bank provides simple funds transfer services and payment guarantees in the form of L/Cs. Its role may be direct or may involve an intermediary bank. While paying under an L/C, it effectively becomes a financier for the importer until the funds are reimbursed. It may even choose to directly finance the entire import operation. It also faces the commercial credit risk of the importer and the risk associated with foreign exchange rate fluctuations.

The exporter's bank acts as intermediary between the exporter and the importer or the L/C issuing bank. It can help in the transfer of funds in simple payment terms as well as act as an agent of the exporter in documentary collection or payment under L/C. It may confirm the L/C and assume payment obligations according to the tenor of the draft. It may negotiate the collection rights and responsibilities for the bill of exchange with the exporter at a discount. In case of either confirming L/C or negotiating a bill of exchange, the bank becomes a financier until the draft matures.

The following diagram (Figure 16) depicts the international trade life cycle and shows where each product comes into play and at what stage financing needs for the importer and the exporter may arise.

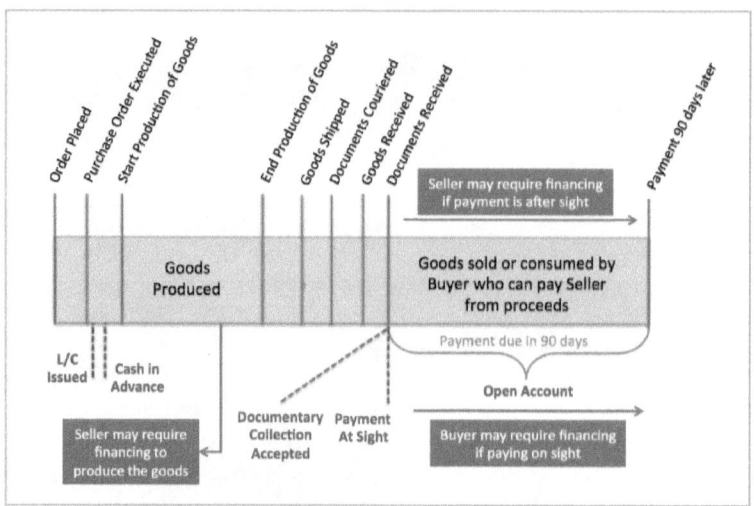

Figure 16

Typically, when the payment becomes due under international trade, the buyer may want to finance the payment depending on his cash flow situation. The buyer may want financing until he is able to sell the goods and collect the funds so he is able to pay the bank. Likewise, if the Draft is a time draft (also known as a Usance draft), the seller may want to get access to the funds as soon as possible rather than wait 30, 60 or 90 days past the presentation and acceptance of the Draft.

Under the basic form of L/C we encountered earlier, the bank plays the role of a middleman between the buyer and the seller helping in mitigating the risks involved. The bank only deals with the documents presented by the seller to ensure they conform to the requirements mentioned in the L/C. Thus, the bank does not own the underlying products involved in an L/C. In addition, if the importer wants financing to be able to pay the exporter, the bank provides financing to the importer and charges interest. Note that if the B/L is consigned to the bank, the bank becomes the actual owner briefly until it consigns it to the buyer. But generally, banks do not want to take ownership of goods but do so only in case of buyer's default.

The fact that the banks generally do not own the goods (unless the B/L is consigned to the bank) and the fact that the bank charges interest in financing cause an out-and-out conflict with Shariah requirements. So, let's take a look at how Islamic financing for international trade resolves these conflicts.

The following table (Figure 17) depicts the most common financing products

78

used in conventional banking vis-a-vis their Islamic banking counterparts at various stages in a production cycle, which we have seen earlier.

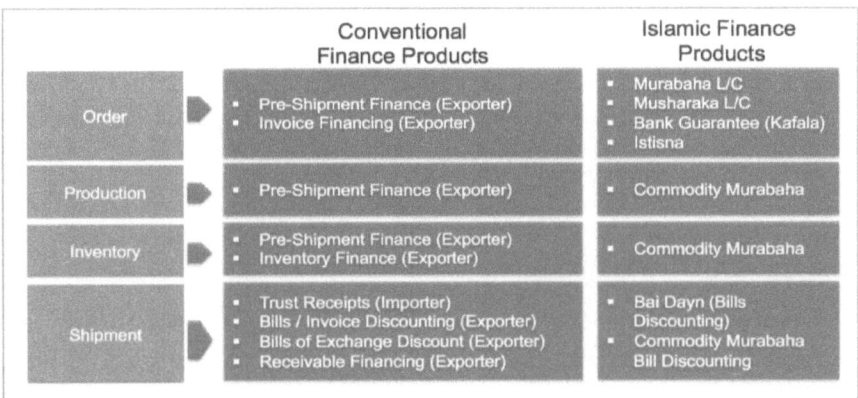

Figure 17

One thing you may notice right away is that the financing product names under Islamic banking are actually the names of trade products. For e.g.: Murabaha L/C sounds like a letter of credit product that is used in international trade. Under conventional banking, the L/C is simply an instrument of trade to mitigate payment risk and other risks associated with international trade as we have seen before. If financing is required, other financing products are used. For e.g.: an exporter may use a financing product called Pre-Shipment Finance for Working capital finance or Invoice Discounting product to finance his receivables. This is a completely separate transaction from the trade transaction like the Letter of Credit or a Documentary Collection (even though they may be linked together). If the exporters have enough funds to pay under the L/C or under the Collections, they may not seek financing at all.

Therefore, under conventional banking an L/C or Documentary Collection is used to facilitate international trade and a separate transaction is created to provide financing if needed. The decision for financing may be made separately outside of the actual trade transaction. For e.g.: in the case of working capital financing, the L/C may be used for pre-shipment financing. In the case of post-shipment finance, the invoice may be used for discounting. Also, the decision to seek financing may be made much later in the process. For eg: the buyer may decide to seek financing after taking possession of the goods and when the payment is due which could be much later.

This works under conventional banking because the bank is simply providing financing and charging interest based on the invoice or the L/C and looking at the credit worthiness of the customer.

However, under Islamic banking this is not possible. If the L/C is issued as a conventional product and financing is sought later, this will not work because under Islamic banking, the bank cannot just provide financing. If you recollect from previous discussions, banks can only provide financing if they first own the goods and then sell the goods to the buyer. As we have seen earlier, under conventional banking, the buyer may have taken possession of the goods already before seeking financing.

Therefore, under Islamic banking, the L/C must be issued following the Shariah guidelines where the bank becomes the owner of the goods so that it may then sell the goods to the buyer and be able to provide financing.

Without the first part where the bank is involved in owning the goods, the second part of financing is not possible.

Issuing the L/C following Shariah requirements in the first part will set the stage for later financing. The buyer still has the option of not seeking any financing. However, if the buyer decides to seek financing, issuing the L/C conforming to Shariah is required in the first step. The product used for this type of financing is known as Goods Murabaha L/C.

Note: the Goods Murabaha is only applicable for L/Cs where the payment terms are defined as sight. Meaning the payment is due immediately when the goods are delivered and the documents are received (Bill of Lading etc.). This is because, this is the only time where it makes sense for the bank to own title to the goods and can sell to the buyer and provide financing.

If the L/C is a Usance L/C, the buyer is not obligated to pay the seller until the due date which is 30 or 90 days (or more) after he typically takes possession of the goods.

In this scenario, the bank owning the goods so it can sell to the buyer on Day1 does not make sense since the buyer is not obligated to pay until 30 or 60 or 90 days anyway. Normally the financing need arises when the payment becomes due, in this scenario, at 30 or 60 or 90 days later. Thus, if the bank owns the goods and sells them to the buyer immediately upon receiving the goods, a deferred payment cannot be set up since the Buyer may not know if they need financing when the payment becomes due. And the bank cannot set up the deferred payment later when the payment becomes due since by that future date the goods would have already been in the possession of the buyer.

Therefore, for L/Cs with Usance terms, a different product called Commodity Murabaha is used instead of Goods Murabaha (more on this below).

There are several options for financing Trade under islamic Banking. We will look at these next.

Financing International Trade under Islamic Banking

We will be reviewing some commonly used financing techniques used in international trade under Islamic finance. Some of these financing options include conventional Letter of Credit products that are modified by combining them with other Islamic contracts to make them compatible with Shariah and to enable financing. These products are:

1. Goods Murabaha (also known as Murabaha L/C)
2. Commodity Murabaha (also known as Tawarruq)
3. Wakala L/C
4. Musharaka L/C
5. Bank Guarantee (Kafalah)
6. Shipping Guarantee (Kafalah)
7. Trust Receipts (Murabaha)
8. Bank Guarantees (Kafalah)
9. Accepted Bills (Bai Al-Dayn)
10. Ijarah (Leasing)

Note: there are many products available under Islamic finance…only the most common ones are listed above.

Goods Murabaha (also known as Murabaha L/C)

If you recall from previous discussion, Murabaha is a simple cost plus profit sale where the seller discloses the cost price plus a profit margin to the buyer. Under Murabaha the payment must be immediate. However, if deferred payment (financing) is required, the deferred payment contract BBA or Bai Muajjal is employed. You may also recall that in order to offer financing, an important requirement under Murabaha is that there should be a sale of goods (the seller just cannot lend money) and that the seller of goods must "own" the goods before they can sell them. Therefore, under Murabaha L/C, the bank must buy the goods from the exporter first and then sell them to the importer.

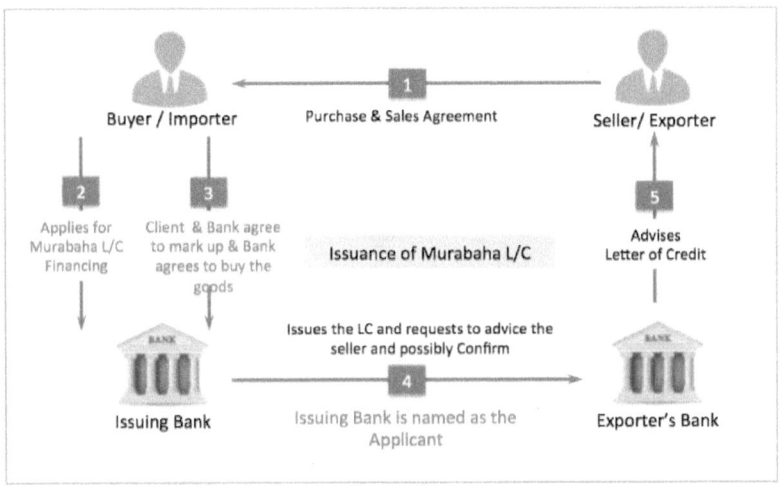

Figure 18

How does this work? Looking at the L/C issuance flow diagram above (figure 18), one can notice a few differences in process flows immediately between Murabaha L/C and a conventional L/C (refer to Figure 15). First of all, the buyer applies for a Murabaha L/C instead of a conventional L/C. Next, the buyer and the bank agree on the markup at which the bank will sell the goods to the buyer once it obtains them from the exporter (step 3 above). The cost price the bank pays is obvious to the buyer since it is the buyer who negotiated the agreement with the exporter in the first place (step 1 above).

Another major difference is that the Issuing bank names itself as the Applicant (buyer) instead of the Importer (actual Buyer). Why? Because the bank has to become the "owner" of the goods, which then enables the bank to sell them to the importer with a markup known as profit. Notice that as far as the Seller (exporter) is concerned, the only difference he will see is that the bank is named as the buyer instead of the actual buyer. There are no other differences from his perspective. This is an important point because Murabaha L/C does not require both the buyer and the seller agree to be part of Islamic contract. As far as the seller is concerned, Murabaha L/C performs and behaves just like a conventional L/C.

Now, let's see what happens when the goods are shipped and the payment is to be made and financing is to be availed.

As can be seen from the following diagram, there is a significant difference is payment under Murabaha L/C v/s conventional L/C. Let's follow this step by step:

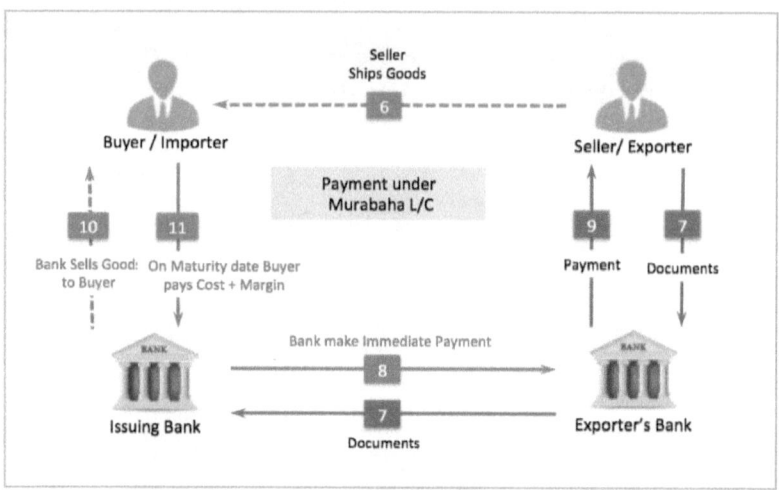

Figure 19

Looking at the L/C payment flow diagram above (figure 19), one can notice a few differences in process flows immediately between Murabaha L/C payment flow and a conventional L/C payment flow. Note that steps 1 thru 4 are not shown here as they are the same as in conventional Payment flow (refer to Figure 14).

Step 6 – the exporter ships the goods either to the Buyer / Importer or the Issuing Bank since the bank is named as the Applicant. The Bank "owns" the goods even if they are directly shipped to the buyer (step 5 in figure 16 is replaced by Step6 here).

Step 7 – generally, the exporter sends the documents to the exporter's bank who then couriers them to the issuing bank.

Steps 8 & 9 – After examining the documents, if the documents agree with the conditions mentioned in the L/C, the Issuing bank immediately makes a payment to the buyer via Exporter's bank if payment is due at sight.

Step 10 – Issuing bank then sells the goods to the buyer under the deferred payment sale (BBA or Bai Muajjal).

Step 11 – on maturity date, the buyer makes cost + margin payment to the Issuing bank that was agreed upon in the beginning. Note: the buyer makes the payments either in lump sum when due or in installments depending on the agreement reached in the beginning.

Even at a quick glance this process is very different from a conventional L/C. There are several key elements that make this Murabaha L/C viable under Shariah. First of all, the bank by naming itself as the Applicant takes ownership of the goods. Note: that it does not have to take "possession" of the goods as long as it "owns" the goods and is responsible for whatever happens to them. That means the bank is basically taking on the risk if something were to happen to the goods.

The second key element is that the bank is selling the goods by declaring what the bank has paid for the goods (the cost) and the profit margin to the buyer. There is no ambiguity here.

Thirdly, both the parties know exactly what is being sold and bought and the terms are clearly agreed upon. This satisfies the Murabaha part of the transaction.

From a financing point of view, the bank is employing the BBA or Bai Muajjal contract that is basically a deferred payment (credit sale) contract. As we have seen before, the basic requirements of BBA or Bai Muajjal contract are:

a) BBA or Bai Muajjal must be used to buy commodities only. Our L/C scenario meets this requirement. Check
b) The due date must be fixed. Check
c) The profit margin is clearly stated. Check
d) Requirement that the buyer should not have already bought the commodity. Check
e) Banks must take precaution and execute all the contracts sequentially. Check

The deferred payment financing under Goods Murabaha L/C meets the basic guideline of BBA or Bai Muajjal.

Murabaha L/C with Buyer as the Agent
A slight variation to the above-described Murabaha L/C process is where the importer's bank (buyers bank) appoints the buyer himself to act as the agent on behalf of the bank through a Master Agency Agreement. This approach may be appropriate where the customer requires specialized goods and is in a better position to verify the specifications of the goods being bought than the bank. This arrangement may also if the goods require specialized storage facilities,

which the buyer may have but the bank may not. Or, it could also be a situation in case of recurring trade financing transactions where the bank does not have to get involved in each and every transaction.

Upon arrival of the goods and the valid stipulated documents, the bank pays the exporter and takes possession of the goods and turns around and sells the goods to the buyer on a cost plus profit basis to be paid by the buyer on cash or on deferred payment basis.

It is interesting to note how the relationship between the bank and its customer changes from one phase to another under this structure. In the first phase when the agreement is reached between the bank and the importer, the relationship between them is that of a Promisee and Promisor since there is no sales contract yet. It then changes into a principal-agent relationship wherein the importer is acting on behalf of the bank in sourcing and verifying the specifications of the goods. In the third phase, it becomes a contract between a seller and a buyer when the bank sells the goods to the buyer. And finally, when the sale is on a deferred payment basis, it is a creditor-debtor relationship.

Therefore, it is important that at each stage the bank and buyer roles, rights, obligations and their implications are distinctly understood. And these separate contracts must be executed separately even if they are executed within a short span of time. If the contracts are executed out of sequence, this transaction may not meet the requirements under Shariah.

You may be wondering how it is possible the above scenario meets the Shariah requirement especially since it is the buyer who is making all the decisions related to selecting the suppliers, selecting the goods and buying them. One must keep in mind that, even though the buyers are directly involved in the sourcing process, they are actually acting as an agent for the bank under the L/C part of the contract. Therefore, any decision the buyer makes, they are making on behalf of the bank. Thus, this arrangement is still legitimate under Shariah since in the initial stage under the L/C contract the bank is still taking the entire risk and becoming the owner of the goods.

Areas where Murabaha L/C can be applied.
Murabaha L/Cs are presently used to finance purchase of fixed assets such as, land, buildings, equipment, automobiles, computers, furniture and the like.

Commodity Murabaha (also known as Tawarruq)
The purpose of this product is to facilitate financing under Usance Letters of Credit or to provide financing where there is no underlying trade activity (as under Goods Murabaha) where a business is simply looking to get financing for

other purposes. That is, this is to provide financing where there is no trade activity which basically equates to lending money. Since, Shariah does not allow just lending money without an underlying trade activity, this option combines several products to achieve this goal.

Under this product the bank will buy commodities from the local commodity market (usually, metals) and sell it to customer at cost plus profit basis with payment due in installments. The customer turns around and sells this commodity to another party for the same cost price the bank paid and gets the required cash.

As mentioned above, one example where Commodity Murabaha is used is in international trade where the seller ships the goods on Usance terms (that is, payment is due 30 or 60 or 90 (or more) days after the buyer receives goods. As stated earlier, in this scenario, it does not make sense for the bank to own the goods and sell to the buyer when goods arrive, since the payment is not due until 30 or 60 days later and the Buyer may not know if they need financing then. Therefore, if the need arises for financing after the Buyer took possession of the goods, the bank can still provide financing using Commodity Murabaha model.

Another area where Commodity Murabaha is used is in pre-shipment finance or working capital finance where the exporter needs financing for short term financing (under 1 year) to buy raw materials or equipment and machinery to be used in the manufacturing of goods.

The bank can use the confirmed purchase order from the buyer as an indication of a valid sale and agree to finance the exporter for working capital. Since the exporter is not buying any goods and may only be buying raw material to make the goods, the bank cannot buy the goods and sell them to the exporter (as under Murabaha L/C). So, instead the bank buys another commodity (mostly metals) and sells this to the buyer for cost plus profit under deferred payment terms. Thus, this part of the transaction becomes a Murabaha sale (a simple cost plus profit deferred payment sale). Next, the exporter sells the commodity to another broker on a cash sale and gets the cash he is looking for. Alternatively, the exporter may appoint another bank as his agent to sell the commodity and get the cash he actually needs to buy raw materials.

Refer below diagram (figure 20) for a detailed explanation of the process involved.

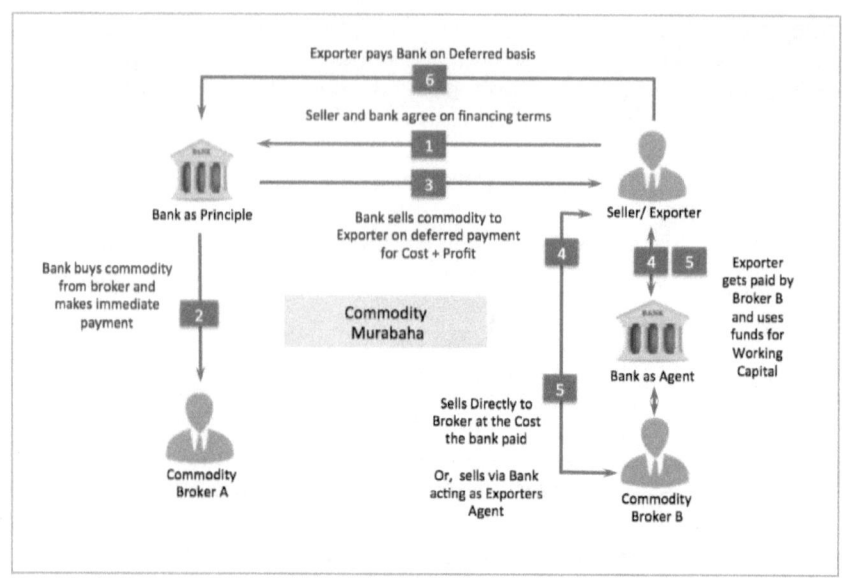

Figure 20

The following is an explanation of the step-by-step process:

Step 1 – the exporter (seller) and his bank agree to the financing terms. This is called Offer and Acceptance and is an important step in this process. It's an offer by the bank to sell the commodity to the seller and an acceptance by the seller to buy the commodity from the bank. The acceptance is important from the bank's perspective for two reasons. One is because the bank does not want to get stuck with the commodity if the exporter changes his mind. The second reason is because the offer lists all the terms of the contract and acceptance by the exporter is important.

Step 2 – the exporter's bank acting as Principal bank buys a commodity from the local market using a commodity Broker A for, let's say $100,000. The commodity itself may be precious metals such as platinum or silver or in some regions palm oil or some other items. At this point the commodity transfers to the bank – that is, the bank owns the commodity and the risk transfers to the bank. This is an important step since the bank cannot sell what it does not own under Shariah. Therefore, the bank must take possession, not necessarily physical possession, but legal possession of the commodity.

Step 3 – Exporter's bank turns around and sells the commodity to the exporter using Murabaha finance product as a deferred payment (Cost + Profit). That is, the bank clearly specifies the cost-plus profit. Note that there are two contracts involved here; a Murabaha contract plus the BBA deferred payment contract although they are combined into one agreement under Murabaha contract. Once the sale is final, the commodity transfers to the exporter. The exporter is obliged to pay the bank the deferred payments as agreed in the contract for the purchase of the commodity.

Steps 4 & 5 – At this point the exporter owns the commodity. And the exporter owes the bank payments on a deferred payment schedule. But the exporter wants cash not commodities. So, the exporter sells the commodity in the local market to another Broker B at the market price (the same $100,000) as cash sale. This is a straightforward sale. The commodity transfers to Broker B. In step 5, Broker B pays the exporter immediately for the commodity if he bought it directly from the exporter. If the exporter employs an agent bank as his agent, Broker B pays the agent bank that then pays the exporter. The exporter now has the cash he is looking for to purchase raw materials or for other manufacturing expenses.

Note that the exporter must sell the commodity to a different broker and not the same broker that the bank used to buy the commodity in the first place as it violates the Shariah principles since this could be construed as a fake transaction (known as Organized Tawarruq). This is because under Shariah, the sale must be genuine. If the same broker is selling the commodity to the bank and buying the same commodity back from the exporter, the object of the sale has no value. It may be considered as a deceptive transaction originated to get quick cash from the transaction. However, if the commodity is sold to another broker who is a separate entity from the first broker, the overall transaction has legitimacy since the commodity has actually moved from Broker A to Broker B via the bank and the exporter. This is known as a 4-corner model. That is there are four separate entities involved in this transaction – the exporter, exporters bank, Broker A and Broker B. And the commodity title is transferred eventually from Broker A to Broker B making it a legit sale.

Optionally, the exporter may appoint another bank as agent and sell the commodity to Broker B thru the agent bank on his behalf. In case an agent bank is appointed, this bank must be a different bank than the bank that sold the commodity to the exporter in the first place.

Step 6 – the exporter makes installment payments to his bank for the terms they originally agreed to.

Under this financing product, in the case of pre-shipment or working capital financing, since the exporter (seller) is looking for financing to buy the raw materials or for purchasing tools and equipment or for other purposes, the exporter does not have goods to sell. The exporter is simply looking for financing to enable manufacturing. Since the bank cannot buy the goods from the seller (as the goods are not manufactured yet), the bank and the seller have to resort to buying commodities to facilitate financing.

Likewise, even under the scenario where the Importer (the buyer, not the seller) is seeking financing, the bank cannot buy the goods from the seller and re-sell to the buyer as under Goods Murabaha, since the payment to seller is not due until 30 or 60 days later. The bank cannot buy the goods and sell to the buyer and expect him to pay at sight (immediately) or sell on deferred payment because the buyer may not know if there would be a need to finance until later. Therefore, under this scenario where the buyer (the importer) wants financing, the bank also utilizes Commodity Murabaha product to facilitate the financing. The possession of the goods involved is not material here since the buying and selling of the commodity acts like the trade activity.

The Commodity Murabaha is used also for financing where trade is not involved. For eg: if a Company is looking for financing to expand its business or for any other reason, the Commodity Murabaha model may be used to facilitate such financing.

In addition, Commodity Murabaha is also used to finance invoices under Supply Chain Finance products. Supply Chain Finance (also known as SCF) is widely used financing product that helps suppliers to get paid early by discounting the invoices. Under this program, the bank uses the buyer's credit worthiness to discount the invoices instead of the sellers. Similar to other scenarios mentioned above, the bank buys and sells commodities to facilitate this financing irrespective of the underlying trade activity.

Musharaka L/C
Musharaka L/C works very much like a regular L/C, wherein a letter of credit is issued in favor of a beneficiary (exporter) on behalf of the applicant (importer) by the bank. The difference is, Musharaka L/C works like a limited partnership between the Bank and the importer who need to import goods and equipment but does not have the sufficient resources to fund the transaction.

In this type of transaction, the importer is required to provide a certain portion of the cost required to purchase the goods and the bank to provide the remaining funds. Upon deposit of the importer's share of funds with the bank, the bank issues the L/C to facilitate the import of the goods. After shipment of the goods and submission and examination of the stipulated documents, the bank makes full payment to the exporter, using the importer's funds and the bank's own funds for the balance. The importer takes possession of the goods and after the importer sells them, the bank and the importer share the profit at a pre-agreed ratio.

The importer may also purchase the bank's share of the imported goods at the market price (cost plus) and thereby buys out the bank's investment. The bank would have made profit since it sold its share of the goods at market price rather than the cost price. The bank may sell its share of the goods to the importer as cash sale or as a deferred payment sale. With this, the importer basically converted a Musharaka sale (partnership) into a Murabaha sale (cost plus profit deferred payment sale).

Wakala L/C

Under Wakalah L/C, the bank acts as the agent of the importer. The importer deposits funds with the bank the full amount of the L/C as collateral to cover the import transaction and the bank issues the L/C. After shipment of goods and submission of stipulated documents by the exporter, the bank makes payment using the buyer's collateral deposit. The bank charges a fee or commission for its services.

Thus, this is not truly a financing product since the bank is not providing any financing. The buyer already deposited the money with the bank at the beginning and the bank is simply using the money deposited by the buyer to make the payment. This is simply a service provided by the bank for which it charges fees or commission.

Bank Guarantee (Kafalah)

Based on the Kafalah concept, this is a product whereby the Bank undertakes to pay the beneficiary the agreed sum, if the applicant fails or defaults in fulfillment of his obligations under the terms and conditions of the contract or agreement with the beneficiary. A Bank Guarantee is an irrevocable obligation, and non-cancellable obligation.

Bank guarantees carry a risk for the issuing bank, which becomes liable to pay out against the guarantee in the event of default by the applicant. Accordingly, the bank takes a liability risk and will first assess the applicant's financial position before issuing any guarantee, in order to determine whether the client's reputation and creditworthiness warrants the bank taking a risk on the performance of the client. In some cases, the bank may ask the applicant to deposit a collateral as security to minimize the risk. These administrative expenses incurred in the process of issuing a guarantee justify the commission charged by the bank.

Islamic banks calculate the commission as a fixed amount on the guaranteed amount without taking into account the period of the guarantee (that is, the duration of the guarantee), as opposed to under conventional finance where the banks calculate guarantee commission based on the guaranteed amount and duration of the guarantee.

The common types of guarantees are bid bond, performance bond, advance payment guarantee, shipping guarantee (see below) and standby letters of credit.

A bid bond, which is a type of guarantee, is issued by a bank on behalf of its client (applicant) who is bidding to secure a contract. The bid bond guarantees that a bidder will not submit an unrealistic bid or, after winning the bid, fails to enter into an agreement.

A performance bond is commonly used in transactions for supply and delivery of goods and services. It guarantees the performance of certain specified acts by the client. If the client fails to perform according to the contract, the bank is obligated to get those acts performed according to the guaranteed commitments.

A standby letter of credit is a guarantee used as a payment of last resort in case the client fails to fulfill a contractual commitment with a third party. It is often used in international trade transactions that don't involve trade L/Cs. Standby letters of credit are usually created as a sign of good faith in business dealings and are proof of an importer's credit quality and repayment ability. The exporter may ask for a standby letter of credit, against which immediate payment can be demanded if the importer fails to make payment by the date specified in the contract.

Shipping Guarantee (Kafalah)
Shipping Guarantee refers to a written indemnity given by the buyer and countersigned by the bank (a guarantee), to the carrier or its agents to allow them to release the goods to the consignee named in the Bill of Lading without presenting the original Bill of Lading. With this guarantee, the bank assures the shipping company that the bank will bear joint liability in case someone else presents the shipping documents to the carrier for the goods.

As we discussed earlier, bill of lading is a critical document that conveys title to the goods and the carrier does not release the goods without evidence of the bill of lading and other shipping documents. In cases where the goods arrive before the Bill of Lading, the goods may be sitting on the ship or in a warehouse waiting to be picked up incurring costs. In such cases, shipping guarantees help importers pick up the goods and avoid such charges while they are waiting for the documents to arrive and are examined.

The process;
1. If the goods arrive at port prior to the documents under L/C or collection, the importer submits the shipping guarantee application (written indemnity) to the bank.

2. After strict examination, the bank offers the shipping guarantee for the importer.

3. The importer picks up the goods from the shipping company (or other carriers) by presenting a shipping guarantee issued by the bank.

4. When documents under L/C or collection arrive, the importer exchanges the shipping guarantee for the original bill of lading with the shipping company (or other carriers) and returns it to the bank.

Under Islamic finance, this works using the concept of Kafalah where it is a contract of guarantee or surety given by one party to discharge the liability of a third party in the case of default.

Trust Receipts (Murabaha)
Islamic Trust Receipts (TR) is a financing product to finance raw materials or semi-finished products or when the buyers take delivery of goods and have to pay the sellers. Under TR, the bank pays the seller and takes ownership of the goods but employs the Buyer as an agent of the bank to sell the goods to a third party. As the goods are sold, the Buyer will pay the bank for what is due. TRs are provided under the Islamic Shariah principle of Tawarruq. The difference under this being, the bank buys the commodity involved in the trade activity instead of some other commodity as in Commodity Murabaha where the underlying trade commodity is not available to the bank.

Bank Guarantee (Kafalah)
Bank Guarantee is a guarantee provided by the bank to the seller who has placed his goods with the buyer (customer of the bank) whereby the bank guarantees payment to the seller using the concept of Kafalah.

Accepted Bill (Murabaha/Bai Al-Dayn)

Islamic Accepted Bill is a trade facility to finance imports or purchase and export of sales. There are two types of Accepted Bills (AB) financing:

1. Accepted Bills Import/Purchase: It can be used for both sight and usance bill of exchange drawn by the Bank on the customer and accepted by the customer to finance import/purchase. This is issued based on the Murabaha contract.

2. Accepted Bills Export/Sales: It is used only for a usance bill of exchange drawn by the customer and accepted by the Bank to finance export/sales. It is issued based on the Bai Al Dayn contract.

Ijarah (leasing)

Buying of equipment, land and buildings and machinery is an important aspect of doing business. It also is a major commitment of funds for many businesses. Therefore, financing makes it possible for businesses to acquire the asset without the need to invest and tie up capital that could be used for other purposes.

Leasing is another form of asset acquisition that allows a business to use an asset or property owned by another party. Lease arrangements can be a simple rental agreement or more elaborate contractual arrangements where the asset transfers to the lessee over time (known as lease to purchase).

Under Islamic finance, Ijarah is an increasingly popular Shariah compliant financial structure in all forms of asset financing. It is a mode of finance where the Islamic bank purchases an asset or equipment at the request of a client and leases it to the client at a price that includes a fair return for the bank.

Ijarah was generally used by Islamic banks for financing of consumer goods such as furniture, vehicles and home financing. However, lately it has also found its way into project finance and for asset-based financing in larger and more complex transactions used by businesses. For e.g.: Ijarah agreements are used to finance airplanes, buildings, equipment and other items that businesses need but cannot afford to outlay the huge capital investments at once.

Under the standard Ijarah contract, the client normally rents the item and at the end of the rental agreement, returns the item to the owner. The standard Ijarah contract does not generally provide the option to buy at the end of the lease. If the leaser wishes to purchase the item at the end of the lease term, they could do so using Ijarah with Iqtina (see below).

There are three types of Ijarah contracts that conform to Shariah:

1. Lease without ownership. This is the standard lease that we just discussed above. Banks also use regular re-pricing of the lease to ensure that returns are competitive within the prevailing market.

2. Lease with ownership (Ijarah wa Iqtina). Under this lease agreement, the person who is leasing (the lessee) owns the item at the end of the lease. Under this contract, the lessee approaches a bank with a request to lease a particular asset or property. The bank and the lessee agree to the terms and conditions of the lease. With this verbal agreement in place, the bank playing the role of a lessor buys the asset or a particular piece of property and enters into a leasing contract with the lessee that specifies the amount and interval of the rental payments to be made by the lessee.

   Since the ownership of the asset remains with the bank, the bank is obligated for any repairs and bears all the risks associated with ownership. For e.g.: if the value of the building goes down, the bank bears all the capital losses. The lessee makes the first rental payment on the day he is able to use the item being rented. The transfer of ownership of the asset from the lessor (bank) to the lessee at the end of the leasing period should be independent of the lease agreement and executed at different phases of the Ijarah contract. According to Shariah, the transfer of ownership in an Ijarah leasing contract may also be done as a gift, but only after the lessee has made all the rental payments. In this case, the lessee and the bank may agree to amortize the cost of the asset as part of the lease. Which means the lessee will pay for the cost of the asset along with the rent as part of the lease payment. This will allow the lessor to transfer the ownership in the asset to the lessee as a gift at the end of the lease since the full value of the asset would have been paid as part of the lease payments.

   The validity of the Ijarah wa Iqtina contract rests on the condition that the lease and sale agreements should be recorded separately (as mentioned above) and only the lessor is obligated to sell at the end of the lease. The lessee is under no obligation to buy.

Conclusion: The future of Islamic Banking

It is true that one of the main reasons why Islamic banking has gained in popularity recently is because of the improving economies of the Muslim countries in Middle East and Asia and the fact that the improving economies are resulting in larger middle class and affluent populations in these regions with bigger wallets and buying power and demanding Islamic banking and finance.

Likewise, the businesses that cater to these populations are growing bigger and demanding Islamic products. This has resulted in increased popularity of Islamic banking products and has forced many local and global banks to take notice and offer Islamic products. This in turn has resulted in a broader awareness of Islamic products among the world populations and not just in the Islamic world.

As people see the benefits that Islamic products offer over conventional products they may choose Islamic products over conventional products in some cases. In addition, the winners and losers concept present in free market economies may entice some businesses to seek Islamic products to mitigate this risk.

Therefore, we expect a bright future for Islamic products irrespective of the retrenchment of investments due to the recent drop in oil prices. Even though economic activity may go up or down depending on what is occurring in the global market, Islamic products are here to stay.

It is our hope that we have convinced you of the benefits of Islamic finance transaction banking products and that you will consider using Islamic products in addition to conventional products. It is also our hope that Islamic banking products become part of your repertoire of products in your overall portfolio along with conventional products.

About the Authors

Mike Nagavalli currently works in a senior role at a major regional bank inUnited Arab Emirates (UAE). In the past 25 years, Mike has worked in different capacities working in the US for global banks including Bank of America, Wells Fargo and Royal Bank of Scotland. His expertise includes delivering and managing digital channels, managing technical teams, enterprise project management, strategy development, product innovation and trade and cash product management. Mike also has extensive experience in executing strategic initiatives globally including in countries such as US, UK, Singapore, China and Hong Kong and more recently provided leadership for successful integration of multiple platforms as a result of merger between two large scale banks.

Mohamed Mahari has been working at Moody's Analytics Dubai office since 2012 as a Credit and Islamic Finance Trainer. He has more than 12 years of experience covering Islamic and corporate banking. Before joining Moody's, Mohamed worked as a Corporate Banker in IB Asia (DBS Singapore) handling the Middle East region with a GCC focus. Mohamed has an extensive knowledge of Islamic banking and finance. Besides being active in delivering Credit and Islamic finance training in the Middle East, he also has a busy schedule delivering Islamic finance training in countries like Singapore, Malaysia, London and UAE.